FLOURISHING
IN AN UNCERTAIN WORLD

WISDOM AND STRATEGIES FROM
PROFESSIONALS AROUND THE WORLD

ENDORSED BY
DR. TAL BEN-SHAHAR
BEST-SELLING AUTHOR OF *HAPPIER*

FLOURISHING IN AN UNCERTAIN WORLD
WISDOM AND STRATEGIES FROM PROFESSIONALS AROUND THE WORLD

Copyright 2025 by North Star Success Inc. All Rights Reserved.

For permission requests and bulk orders, please contact support@northstarsuccess.com.

North Star Success Inc. is hereby identified as the owner of this work in accordance with Section 77 of the Copyright, Design and Patents Act 1988.

ISBN: 978-1-0691324-7-5

No part of this publication may be scanned, reproduced, stored in a retrieval system, or transmitted, in any form or by any means, electronic, mechanical, photocopying, recording or otherwise, for public or private use – other than as brief quotations embodied in articles and reviews – without the prior consent of North Star Success Inc. This book is sold subject to the condition that it shall not, by way of trade or otherwise, be lent, resold, hired out or otherwise circulated without North Star Success's prior consent in any form of binding or cover other than that in which it is published.

This is a work of non-fiction. Any resemblance of names, personal characteristics, and details of people, living or dead, is coincidental and unintentional. The authors are responsible for their content and their opinions. AI tools have been used to translate and edit the author-created content. All AI-translated and/or AI-assisted content adheres to all content guidelines.

The reader is solely responsible for their actions and results. If professional or legal advice is required, readers should seek the service of a competent professional. For bulk orders for promotions, fundraising, and educational use, please contact North Star Success Inc. for special discounts. Book excerpts can be created as needed.

Trademark Notice: All brand names and product names used in this book are trademarks, registered trademarks, or trade names of their respective holders. North Star Success Inc. is not associated with any product or vendor mentioned in this book.

Published by North Star Success Inc.

🌐 www.northstarsuccess.com
✉ support@northstarsuccess.com
📞 +1 647 479 0790

"Flourishing in an Uncertain World" is replete with evidence-based advice that can help you lead a happier, healthier life. Integrating inspiring stories and rigorous research, this book can change your life for the better.

Dr. Tal Ben-Shahar
Author, Lecturer, Former Harvard University Professor and Leading Voice in the Field of Positive Psychology
Author of the International Bestseller, *Happier*

Dr. Tal Ben-Shahar is a world-renowned author, lecturer, and expert in the fields of positive psychology and leadership. He taught one of the most popular courses in Harvard University's history on "Positive Psychology." Through his international bestsellers, including *Happier* and *Being Happy*, he provides practical, evidence-based frameworks for leading a more joyful and fulfilling life. His work is dedicated to helping people move from simply succeeding to truly flourishing.

Contents

Foreword.. 9

Introduction... 13

Banafsheh Amiraslani
Scientific Perspective
A Flourishing Brain
Strategies to Boost Brain Strength.................................17

Dr. Mostafa Azimi
But Why Now?
Rebuilding the Wheel of Life for Growth and Flourishing.......... 47

Negar Dianat
From Foreign Lands to Inner Truth
A Journey Toward Flourishing: From Immigration
to Identity Restoration in an Unstable World............................... 65

Shervin Esfandyari
The Art of Flourishing
Meaning, Growth, and Resilience When Life Isn't Easy.............. 81

Amirhossein Hajigholami
A Home Across the Waters
Flourishing Through Future-Minded Property Investment.......... 97

Maryam Kai Kabir
The Power of Small, Sustainable, and Consistent Changes
An Inner Wave—Gentle Yet Powerful—that Begins with the
Tiniest Drop and Flows Toward Sustainable Flourishing........... 115

Mohsen Khaki
From Surviving to Thriving
A Coaching Guide to Flourishing at Work and Beyond...............135

Mohammad Mehri
Shining in the Heart of Darkness
Navigating a Foggy Path When
Only Your Inner Light Illuminates the Way.................................155

Marjan Shams
That Which You Dread Is Where You're Led............................. 169

Dr. Alireza Talebian
The Star I Couldn't Find in the Sky
From Cosmic Questions to Inner Light: A Journey
toward Flourishing.. 187

Foreword

There are moments in life when an idea is born that feels not just timely but essential. This book, "Flourishing in an Uncertain World," is one of them. For years, we have been told that the key to success is resilience—the ability to bounce back from adversity. We've been praised for our capacity to endure, to survive, and to rebuild. But what if we are meant to do more than recover?

This book introduces the concept of flourishing as the actual engine of sustained high performance and lasting fulfillment. Flourishing isn't about denying hardship; it's about using it as a catalyst for growth. The authors of this book—a diverse collective of experts from fields as varied as medicine, law, engineering, and psychology—guide us on a journey from surviving to thriving. They present a holistic, evidence-based roadmap that challenges the traditional narratives of success.

Through a powerful combination of personal stories and scientific insight, this book offers a new lens for understanding ourselves and the world. You'll learn from a brain health coach who provides a scientific blueprint for a flourishing brain, explaining how nurturing our mental well-being is the foundation for all growth. You will see how a legal expert uses a fictional narrative to underscore the dangers of regret and how a health coach's journey of immigration and anxiety can become a source of strength. A clinical psychologist shares how to transform pain into a source of strength, while a strategic consultant reveals how to achieve "purposeful wealth" through international property investment.

Other contributors offer their unique perspectives from the front lines of life and work. An author and coach shows how the quiet force of small, consistent changes can lead to monumental transformation. A professional coach uses case studies to demonstrate that organizations and individuals thrive when they invest in personal development, not just resilience. A flight engineer and mental clarity coach shares his personal journey of finding purpose by paying attention to the subtle signs along the way. You will also discover how to transform fear from an enemy into a powerful guide, learning to embrace uncertainty and trust your own wisdom. And finally, a physicist specializing in astronomy and gravity shows how the quest for a cosmic purpose can ultimately lead to profound human connection.

This book is a testament to the idea that our most significant breakthroughs often lie on the other side of our fears and our discomfort. It's an invitation to shift your perspective and build a life that is not just successful, but deeply meaningful.

Dr. Tal Ben-Shahar, a leading voice in the science of happiness, has endorsed the work within these pages. As he notes, this book is "replete with evidence-based advice that can help you lead a happier, healthier life. Integrating inspiring stories and rigorous research, this book can change your life for the better."

It is with immense pride that we present "Flourishing in an Uncertain World." It is a book born from a profound moment of global uncertainty, and it is here to guide you toward a future of unwavering purpose, strength, and joy.

Dr. Katayoon Bidad
Co-founder of North Star Success Publishing Company

Introduction

In an era defined by volatility, uncertainty, complexity, and ambiguity, the demands on professionals and leaders have never been greater. The traditional markers of success are being redefined in real-time, and the pressure to perform is relentless. For years, our conversations about navigating this landscape have centered on a crucial concept: resilience. We have rightly celebrated resilience as the vital capacity to withstand pressure, recover from setbacks, and adapt to change. It is the bedrock of durability.

But as our understanding of human potential deepens, we are compelled to ask a more ambitious question: Is durability the ultimate goal? Is returning to our baseline after a shock sufficient for those who seek not just to survive in this new world, but to excel within it?

This is where the paradigm must shift—from the reactive stance of resilience to the proactive, generative state of flourishing. This book, Flourishing in an Uncertain World, is an invitation to make that essential shift. It posits that

INTRODUCTION

flourishing is not a soft ideal, but the very engine of sustained, high performance.

Flourishing, as explored within these pages, is a holistic concept deeply rooted in the science of positive psychology. It moves beyond mere survival to address the core components of a thriving life: cultivation of positive emotions, the pursuit of meaning and purpose, the deep engagement found in a state of 'flow,' the nurturing of positive relationships, and the sense of accomplishment that comes from true mastery. It argues that creativity, innovation, and effective leadership are not outcomes to be pursued in spite of pressure, but natural results of a system—a person, a team, an organization—that is truly flourishing.

This book does not offer a simple list of habits or quick fixes. Instead, it provides stories and ideas about the concept of whole person wellbeing. It challenges us to move beyond problem-focused questions like, "How do I prevent burnout?" to potential-focused inquiries such as, "How can we leverage our innate character strengths to create value and find fulfillment in our work?" This is a fundamental shift from mitigating weakness to amplifying strengths—a cornerstone of building both individual and collective capacity.

The stories in this book uplift and inspire you. They will provide you with the frameworks to build what positive psychology calls 'psychological capital'—the powerful combination of hope, self-efficacy, and optimism. You will meet individuals that have faced uncertainty not as a threat to be endured, but as a catalyst for their own development and achievement.

The future of performance will not be defined by who can endure the most, but by who can flourish the most. This book provides ideas and inspiration for that essential and rewarding journey toward a life of purpose, engagement, and lasting impact.

Dr. Shahab Anari
ICF Master Coach (MCC),
Founder of North Star Coach Training Program

Scientific Perspective

A Flourishing Brain
Strategies to Boost Brain Strength

Banafsheh Amiraslani

Scientific Perspective

A Flourishing Brain
Strategies to Boost Brain Strength

Banafsheh Amiraslani
Brain Health Coach and Flourishing Instructor

Do you recall a challenging time not so long ago, when an uninvited guest, the Coronavirus, brought about dramatic changes all over the world in our daily lives? A tiny but disturbing virus just appeared all of a sudden somewhere beyond the boundaries, in the cold December of 2019, spreading swiftly across the globe. The people who had been striving intensely until then, abruptly encountered a pandemic, as if the burning passions for pursuing their goals were seasoned with fear, anxiety, and uncertainty. According to the advice of the World Health Organization (WHO), "staying home" was the best and most preferred solution to remain safe.

The pandemic disrupted the usual flow of life to an incredible extent. It severely impacted the means of communication, dwindling in-person meetings and family gatherings almost to zero. COVID-19 led to the widespread closure of gyms and leisure centers, seriously affecting a significant number of other businesses. Additionally, it shut down numerous educational institutes, schools and universities, turning traditional classrooms, which were once the most common method of education, into a memory carved in minds.

Now the question is: how did people cope with those arduous circumstances and still endeavor to turn their dreams into reality? Thanks to state-of-the-art technologies, specifically intelligent devices and communication platforms, *learning* continued through an alternative method, "online education," and it became possible to access teachers even from miles away. Indeed, the e-learning system provided not only novel opportunities for acquiring knowledge and proficiencies, but also the chance to participate in numerous scientific, national, and international events. Besides, virtual communications formed through attending multi-person learning environments, helped amplify social connections, create new friendships and expand our network of like-minded individuals. Such communications can be invaluable, as they may evolve into subsequent professional collaborations and team-oriented projects.

Here, these questions may arise:

What is the relevance of learning and social connections to the brain?

And how can they assist us on our path toward growth and prosperity?

To address these queries, let's proceed to the next section.

The Impacts of Learning and Communications on the Brain

Learning is an inevitable part of the human journey throughout life. Like an ever-present companion, it is by our side, step by step, from the most basic tasks—such as when a child learns to walk—to far more sophisticated ones, including various sciences and skills, throughout adulthood. We, as human beings, possess an inconceivable capacity for learning, and this feature is one of the factors of our species' success [1]. Within the brain, the hippocampus is a crucial region for various types of learning [2, 3]. Multiple studies have exhibited that the bulk of new neurons is created daily through neurogenesis[1] in the adult hippocampus of varied species, including humans [2-7]. Nonetheless, most of the newborn cells do not survive beyond a few weeks [2-5]. It may sound disquieting, but there is a potent rescuer for keeping these new neurons alive; *learning*, the kind of which is new, challenging and successful [2-5]. The rescued neurons appear to dwell in the hippocampus for several months [3-5]. By then, the differentiation of nearly all salvaged cells has occurred, and they form synapses and express action potentials as they are incorporated into the existing brain circuitry [2, 4, 5].

But how does effortful learning practically occur? One proposed strategy is engaging in some studying approaches,

---

1. Neurogenesis is the process through which new neurons are generated within the brain. Neurogenesis is crucial during embryo development, but it also continues in specific brain areas after birth and throughout our lifespan. Retrieved from: https://qbi.uq.edu.au/brain-basics/brain-physiology/what-neurogenesis

such as spaced learning,[1] self-examination and interleaving[2], which can make learning more strenuous and enhance the likelihood of cells surviving to become functional hippocampal neurons [4, 8].

The survival of recently generated cells through learning is an excellent example of the rule: "use it or lose it" [5]. New cells present during learning are more likely to survive than those not exposed to learning [5]. It is worth noting that the cell-preserving agent is not solely the training experience, but rather the *learning* is a crucial issue that happens during training [3-5].

If you intend to fuel those tiny newborn neurons to outlive and join the brain network, what new learning would satisfy this purpose?

- Learning and Neuroplasticity

The learning process is mediated by neural plasticity, a procedure through which both structural and functional

---

1. "Spaced learning comprises breaking a long course into several sessions or modules of shorter durations with breaks in between the sessions. With this approach of teaching, learners can retain the information taught in the course." Retrieved from: https://www.instancy.com/what-is-spaced-learning

2. Interleaving is a type of learning method by which students mix, or interleave, several subjects or topics while they study to ameliorate their learning. Blocked practice, on the contrary, comprises studying one topic very thoroughly before going to study another one. Interleaving is a more useful technique compared with blocked practice for developing both categorization and problem-solving skills; additionally, interleaving results in better long-term retention and an improved capability of transfering learned knowledge. Retrieved from: https://academicaffairs.arizona.edu/l2l-strategy-interleaving

alterations occur within the adult brain to adapt to changes in external and internal surroundings [9-11]. In accordance with the literature, neuroplasticity exists throughout one's entire life and comprises multiple facets, such as alterations in the morphology of brain regions as well as in neuronal networks, involving modifications of neuronal connectivity, neurogenesis and neurobiochemical changes [11, 12]. Structural alterations induced by learning can also influence anatomical connectivity within the adult brain [9]. It has been claimed that the major structural mechanisms for experience-dependent[1] plasticity are axonal remodelling, the formation of new dendritic spines and synaptic turnover[2] in mature cortex [9, 13]. Learning occurs through the generation of new connections between nerve cells that are activated simultaneously and repeatedly, providing a worthy reminder of the neuroscience principle: "neurons that fire together, wire together" [14, 15]. Once new learning occurs, the involved synapses in this process enhance their efficacy and facilitate subsequent neuronal communication.[3]

---

1. "Experience-dependent is the neural connections that develop in response to experience. In psychology, the term «experience-dependent» refers to the idea that the structure and function of the brain are shaped by experiences that an individual has throughout their lifetime. This concept suggests that the brain is constantly changing and adapting in response to experiences, and that these changes can occur at any age." Retrieved from: https://www.psychology-lexicon.com

2. "Synaptic turnover, a form of structural plasticity, refers to the dynamic process of continuous formation and dismantling of synapses and is strongly associated with learning in multiple areas of the brain" [13].

3. Retrieved from: https://svenschild.com/blog/f/hebbs-law-what-fires-together-wires-together

- Further Benefits of Learning

The advantage of learning also encompasses its contribution to the increment of both gray and white matter in the human brains of adults [9]. In addition, the risk of mental illnesses like cognitive impairment may be diminished by continuous learning/cognitive training [16].[1] Interestingly, learning also plays an effective role in combating brain aging, which is probably a reversible phenomenon [14]. Due to the plastic nature of the brain throughout life, learning experiences have the potential to help its maps restructure themselves [14].

Learning not only has beneficial influences on the brain but also helps individuals broaden their vision and intellectual horizons, strengthen social connections, and encounter inspiring people along life's journey. *Social ties* have been demonstrated to promote both mental and physical well-being [17]. Individuals with greater social support are better equipped to manage vocational stress [17]. Likewise, they are less inclined to experience mental health problems such as depression, anxiety and post-traumatic stress disorder (PTSD) [17]. Repeated stress, in multiple ways, affects the brain, the primary organ that perceives and adapts to stress [18]. Chronic stress induces morphological alterations in neurons across

---

1. "Cognitive training is an approach that seeks to sharpen or maintain brain functions through the use of regular mental activities. These mental activities are intended to help cognitive abilities such as working memory, executive function, and problem-solving abilities." Retrieved from:https://www.verywellmind.com/cognitive-training-long-term-improvement-2795014

diverse brain regions, exacerbates apoptosis,[1] and suppresses adult neurogenesis within the hippocampus, leading to subsequent impaired learning capability and memory function [11, 19, 20].

Keeping in touch with others also has advantageous impacts on chronic disorders, including cognitive decline and dementia.[2] Indeed, enhancing social engagement and preserving emotionally supportive relationships are effective strategies against these age-related health issues [21]. Social interactions can also evoke positive emotions, such as happiness and hope, making us more resolute to actualize our objectives and helping us persevere through times of difficulty [22].

Do positive emotions make any impression on the brain? The response is yes, and the what and the how of this effect are the matter of the following section.

Fortifying the Brain by the Blessing of Positive Emotions

Do you remember a particular occasion when you experienced positive emotions and acted stronger and more creative in

---

1. "Apoptosis is a type of cell death in which a series of molecular steps in a cell lead to its death. This is one method the body uses to get rid of unneeded or abnormal cells. The process of apoptosis may be blocked in cancer cells. Also called programmed cell death." Retrieved from: https://www.cancer.gov/publications/dictionaries/cancer-terms/def/apoptosis
2. "Dementia is a term for several diseases that affect memory, thinking, and the ability to perform daily activities." Retrieved from: https://www.who.int/news-room/fact-sheets/detail/dementia

dealing with challenges and problematic issues?

According to the broaden-and-build theory of Dr. Barbara Fredrickson, joy, interest, contentment, and love, which are categorized as positive emotions, make people's transient reservoir of both thoughts and actions wider, while also constructing their perpetual personal resources, including physical, intellectual, social, and psychological assets [23-25]. This theory, along with other research, recommends that positive emotions have the potential to expand individuals' attention and thinking, make them more healthful and resilient, enhance cognitive flexibility[1] in addition to achieving optimal performance [23, 26, 27]. Besides, diverse cognitive processes, including attention, memory, mental rotation,[2] problem solving and social cognition,[3] as well as creative, pliable, and practical thinking patterns, are all promoted by positive emotions [26, 27].

The brain has a complex emotional circuitry, involving

---

1. "Cognitive flexibility is an intrinsic property of a cognitive system often associated with the mental ability to adjust its activity and content, switch between different task rules and corresponding behavioral responses, maintain multiple concepts simultaneously and shift internal attention between them." Retrieved from: https://en.wikipedia.org/wiki/Cognitive_flexibility

2. "Mental rotation is the ability to rotate mental representations of two-dimensional and three-dimensional objects, as it is related to the visual representation of such rotation within the human mind." Retrieved from https://en.wikipedia.org/wiki/Mental_rotation

3. "Social cognition is a topic within psychology that focuses on how people process, store, and apply information about other people and social situations. It focuses on the role that cognitive processes play in social interactions." Retrieved from: https://en.wikipedia.org/wiki/Social_cognition

cooperative structures in regions such as the prefrontal cortex,[1] amygdala,[2] hippocampus, anterior cingulate cortex,[3] and insular cortex[4] to process and create both emotional data and emotional behavior [28, 29]. It is believed that the dopamine system mediates the abundant impacts that positive emotions exert on both behavior and cognition [26]. Dopamine, a pivotal neurotransmitter, is synthesized in some districts[5] of the brain [30]. Other neurochemicals involved in positive emotions include serotonin, endorphin and oxytocin [31].

---

1. "Prefrontal cortex: The most anterior (forward) part of the cerebral cortex of each frontal lobe in the brain. Divided into a dorsolateral region and an orbitofrontal region, the prefrontal cortex functions in attention, planning, working memory, and the expression of emotions and appropriate social behaviors." Retrieved from: https://dictionary.apa.org/prefrontal-cortex

2. "Amygdala, region of the brain primarily associated with emotional processes. The amygdala is located in the medial temporal lobe, just anterior to (in front of) the hippocampus. The amygdala is part of the limbic system, a neural network that mediates many aspects of emotion and memory." Retrieved from: https://www.britannica.com/science/amygdala

3. The Anterior Cingulate Cortex (ACC), a part of the limbic system, is involved in regulating attention and emotion, inhibitory control as well as error monitoring and motivation [29].

4. The insular cortex (or insula) is a part of the cerebral cortex folded deep within the lateral sulcus, separating the temporal lobe from the parietal and frontal lobes in each hemisphere of the mammalian brain. The insula is believed to be involved in consciousness and diverse functions related to emotion and the regulation of the body's homeostasis. These functions comprise compassion, empathy, taste, perception, motor control, self-awareness, cognitive functioning, interpersonal relationships, as well as awareness of homeostatic emotions such as hunger, pain, and fatigue. In relation to these, it is implicated in psychopathology. Retrieved from: https://en.wikipedia.org/wiki/Insular_cortex

5. "In the substantia nigra, ventral tegmental area and hypothalamus" [30].

Serotonin,[1] a tryptophan[2]-derived neurotransmitter, mediates happiness, satisfaction and optimism [31, 32]. Exposure to the bright light can naturally raise the brain's serotonin levels [33]. Endorphins are opioid neuropeptides, endogenously produced by both the pituitary gland[3] and the hypothalamus [31, 34, 35].[4] These chemicals act as natural painkiller molecules and enhancers of pleasure inside the body [31, 34]. Engaging in continuous exercise, eating chocolate, listening to music, and laughing are some activities that assist in releasing endorphins [31, 34]. Another substance is oxytocin, a nine-amino acid neuropeptide hormone, synthesized within the hypothalamus [31, 36]. Oxytocin provides the ease of connection with others and regulates emotional demeanor, while also stimulating socializing, trust, empathy, and optimistic communication [31, 34].

---

1. Interestingly, over 90% of serotonin is produced in the gut, and this chemical exerts a key function in regulating gut secretion and peristalsis [32].
2. Tryptophan (Trp) is a nutritionally important amino acid that exists in small amounts in proteins. Trp as an essential amino acid, must be obtained from the diet, since humans and certain other animals are not able to synthesize it. Retrieved from: https://www.britannica.com/science/tryptophan
3. The pituitary gland, known as the hypophysis, is a small, pea-sized gland located at the base of the brain, underneath the hypothalamus. This gland is a part of the endocrine system, responsible for making numerous essential hormones. The pituitary gland also controls the function of several other glands of the endocrine system. Retrieved from: https://my.clevelandclinic.org/health/body/21459-pituitary-gland
4. The hypothalamus is a brain region located below the thalamus, forming the floor of the third cerebral ventricle. It serves as a control center for various autonomic functions and influences the endocrine system through its interaction with the pituitary gland. Retrieved from: https://www.britannica.com/science/hypothalamus

In the succeeding paragraphs, several brain-friendly approaches that can eventuate in experiencing pleasant emotions and mental well-being will be discussed in further detail.

Connection with the bounteous nature, this divine blessing, can be a vigorous provenance for provoking the flow of positive emotions. This also plays a part in brain activity, mental health and improved cognitive function [37]. Based upon evidence, human interaction with nature is associated with enhanced positive affect, life satisfaction, vitality, calmness, optimism, gratitude, and the sensation of meaning and purpose in life [38-41]. There is a relationship between exposure to natural settings and alterations in the activity of the prefrontal cortex, a brain area that holds great significance in regulating emotions [37]. A link also exists between the perception of natural scenery and an increase in the activity of the anterior cingulate and insula, the brain regions associated with positive social behavior, such as empathy and altruism [42]. Contact with nature also promotes a greater amount of relaxation and acts as a stimulator of the brain activity associated with tranquility [42]. Besides, it gives rise to higher levels of alpha[1] brain waves over the frontal lobes [42]. Interestingly, watching the videos of nature has the potential to enhance alpha as well as theta[2] power, proposing that natural

---

1. Alpha waves are generally related to the state of mind which is more relaxed and alert [43].
2. Theta oscillations assist with alertness state and the capability of rapid information processing [43].

stimuli arouse a mental state of relaxation yet alertness [42].

Spending time in nature has a restorative effect on mental fatigue associated with modern living, restoring direct attention and mitigating stress and autonomic arousal by activating the parasympathetic nervous system [37, 42].[1,2] The extra benefits of nature exposure include, but are not limited to: a decline in rumination and mental distress, such as negative affect, anxiety and depression, in addition to improvement in cognitive control[3] and concentration [37, 38, 42].

Meditation is considered a booster of positive emotions by augmenting the quantity of both serotonin and dopamine [33, 43, 44]. It is a form of self-regulation exercise, able to ameliorate both mental and emotional control [45]. Through meditation, significant changes occur in the brain, and the centers responsible for emotion and cognition are activated [44]. The correlation of meditation and mental health arises from the fact that meditation-mediated positive emotion helps address diverse mental illnesses such as social anxiety disorder, depression, PTSD and anxiety [44]. During meditation, there is a rise in brain waves,[4] including theta high-frequency power and low alpha frequency within the anterior cerebral regions,

---

1. The Attention Restoration Theory (ART) and the Stress Reduction Theory (SRT), respectively [37, 42].
2. Natural sounds are also capable of refreshing this mental fatigue [42].
3. "Cognitive control orchestrates thoughts and actions in accordance with goals and contexts." Retrieved from: https://psychology.uiowa.edu/cognitive-control
4. It has been shown that the power of alpha and theta brain waves in individuals who have meditated for a great deal of time were higher in comparison with non-meditators [43].

accompanied by a decline and enhancement in the activities of the sympathetic and parasympathetic systems, respectively [43, 45]. There appears to be an inverse correlation between the activity of these brain waves and anxiety disorders; that is, as the activity of alpha and theta waves increases, anxiety levels are alleviated [43]. Interestingly, a distinct type of meditation, known as focused attention meditation, is an effortful learning process, as the meditator learns to reside in the present moment and respond less to arising thoughts and emotions [2].

Accomplishing creative pursuits is another beneficial strategy. Creativity, the ability to generate novel and practical ideas, insights, and solutions, is among the top 10 skills of 2025, as claimed by the World Economic Forum [46, 47]. Multiple areas[1] inside the brain get involved in creativity, an ability which contributes to mental health by decreasing stress, anxiety and depression in particular.[2] Any creative tasks, such as making music, knitting and drawing, can lead to the production of "happy hormone", dopamine, which is a natural anti-depressant chemical. Creating something and gardening are declared to be effective in lessening anxiety. Likewise, creativity exerts a role in being sharp-witted and assists in lowering the risk of dementia and the incidence of

---

1. The prefrontal cortex, the limbic system, the parietal and occipital lobes. Retrieved from: https://online.jwu.edu/blog/unlocking-power-mind-brain-region-behind-creativity-and-imagination/

2. To the end of the paragraph is retrieved from: https://online.jwu.edu/blog/unlocking-power-mind-brain-region-behind-creativity-and-imagination/

mental states such as depression and loneliness as well.

Physical activity, as a robust technique, changes the brain's neurochemistry and ameliorates neural performance [48]. It acts as a trigger for the release of neurotransmitters, including endorphins, serotonin, and dopamine, which play crucial roles in regulating mood and emotions [48]. Exercise helps provoke not only neuroplasticity but also neurogenesis, a phenomenon that enriches the reservoir of neurons for survival during the learning process [4, 48, 49]. In response to exercise, various physiological alterations occur within the brain, including elevated blood flow,[1] the synthesis of brain-derived neurotrophic factor (BDNF),[2] and the release of endorphins, which in turn lead to improvements in brain structure, cognitive function, and mental well-being [48]. Regular exercise can promote the overall health of the brain and exert a protective effect against various neurological diseases, as well as the deleterious effects of aging [48, 49]. Exercise also has the potential to mitigate both inflammation and depression, improve sleep quality, and enhance self-esteem and social support [48].

---

1. Doing exercise incites the growth of new blood vessels within the brain [48]. This can ameliorate blood circulation and oxygenation in the areas of the brain involved in cognitive function, facilitate the transport of nutrients as well as the removal of metabolic byproducts [48].

2. Brain-derived neurotrophic factor (BDNF), as an essential component of neuroplasticity, has a role in promoting neuronal development, survival, and new synapses formation, probably improving cognitive function and providing neuroprotective influence against diseases [48]. Exercise has a role in enhancing brain performance and alleviating depressive symptoms through increasing the amount of BDNF [48].

Numerous other factors, such as gratitude and kindness, spiritual activities, striving to attain goals, and forming profound human connections, are among the triggers of positive emotions [50].

Ultimately, to put these strategies into practice, the closing question of this section is: What action would you choose if you are inclined to experience more positive emotions?

What Are the Neuroprotective Effects of Sleep?

Sleep serves a crucial function in human life, regulating body metabolism, improving memory recall, and lessening mental fatigue [51]. It appears that an essential amount of daily sleep for appropriate cognitive and behavioral performance is a minimum of 7 hours. [51]. Sleep provides the brain with an opportunity to reorganize and recharge itself, while also eliminating toxic waste substances accumulated during wakefulness [51, 52]. There is a precise waste clearance network inside the brain known as the glymphatic system, which is a fluid-filled channel which facilitates the removal of toxins [51]. During sleep, the cerebrospinal fluid (CSF)[1] eliminates the brain's beta-amyloid metabolite, the accumulation of which over time can lead to multiple neurodegenerative disorders, such as Alzheimer's disease

---

1. "Cerebrospinal fluid (CSF) is the clear liquid that surrounds and bathes the brain and spinal cord. It is not only crucial in cushioning the brain and spinal cord and maintaining intracranial pressure but also for the removal of waste products." Retrieved from: https://radiopaedia.org/articles/cerebrospinal-fluid-1

(AD) and dementia [51]. Thus, sleep has the capacity to clear the brain and support its natural function [51]. Of considerable importance is that melatonin, a well-known hormone which regulates the sleep cycle by controlling circadian rhythm, acts as a powerful antioxidant[1] and thus represents protective effects on nerve cells [53, 54]. It is not only capable of directly activating the intracellular antioxidant system but also chelating both oxygen and nitrogen reactive species [53]. Sleep deprivation, on the contrary, leaves devastating impacts not only on mental and physical health, but also on cognitive and body's motor function [51]. Furthermore, it can lead to the malfunction of specific neurons, which in turn affects both the behavior and performance of individuals [51].[2] Sleep helps the body rest and re-energize itself, and in addition to prolonging alertness and memory recall, it also serves as a stress reliever and depression alleviator [51].

The Importance of Nutrients with Emphasis on Antioxidants

Another pivotal element in mental wellness is a healthy nutritional pattern that has a range of impacts, a key part of which is through anti-inflammatory, antioxidant, and neurogenesis mechanisms [55]. The influence of dietary profile

---

1. An antioxidant is any compound able to neutralize unstable molecules known as free radicals. Retrieved from: https://www.health.harvard.edu/staying-healthy/understanding-antioxidants
2. Certain stages of sleep are essential for neuronal regeneration in the cerebral cortex while the other ones are necessary for the formation of new memories as well as the generation of new synaptic connections [51].

encompasses various aspects, ranging from the composition, structure, and function of the brain to endogenous hormones, neuropeptides, neurotransmitters, and the microbiota-gut-brain axis, which in turn contribute to the modulation of stress and inflammation, as well as the preservation of cognitive function [55]. Antioxidant nutrients, which are efficient reducers of oxidative stress[1] by scavenging reactive oxygen species (ROS), are specifically vital for brain well-being [56]. Owing to several features, including an abundance of lipids, a high rate of oxygen consumption, and a low level of antioxidants, the brain is a vulnerable organ to oxidative stress, a condition that negatively affects various biological processes, such as neurogenesis [57-60]. To help combat ROS, the brain is naturally equipped with a potent antioxidant defense system [57, 58].[2] Additionally, dietary antioxidants can make significant contributions to staving off oxidative stress and maintaining redox homeostasis within the brain [57, 58, 61]. Nutritional substances such as curcumin,[3] resveratrol,[4] blueberry polyphenols, and omega-3 polyunsaturated fatty acids (PUFAs) stimulate adult neurogenesis and contribute to the attenuation of oxidative stress and neuroinflammation

---

[1]. Oxidative stress is a situation in which the generation of free radicals exceeds the antioxidant system capacity [63].
[2]. Including both enzymatic and non-enzymatic antioxidants [58, 59].
[3]. Curcumin, a polyphenolic compound, which is abundant in turmeric [60].
[4]. Resveratrol is a stilbenoid, a phenolic compound, present in substances like peanuts, tree nuts, grapes, cocoa, berry fruits and so on [58, 60].

[60, 62]. Besides, vitamin E, ascorbate,[1] carotenoids,[2] and plant phenols[3] are among the powerful antioxidants with neuroprotective properties [58]. Vitamin E protects against lipid peroxidation and enhances the amount of glutathione (GSH)[4] and the activity of various endogenous antioxidant enzymes[5] within the brain tissue [58]. Ascorbate, a major antioxidant within biological systems, seems to have a crucial role in central nervous system (CNS) homeostasis due to its high concentrations in the brain and CSF [57- 59]. Several metals, including copper, manganese, zinc, selenium, magnesium, and iron, are also of great importance due to their significant involvement as components or cofactors of multiple enzymatic antioxidants, in addition to their varied biological functions [57, 59].

To wrap up this section, here is a list of nutritious foods for the brain:[6]

---

1. Ascorbic acid (vitamin C), is also a key co-factor for the synthesis of numerous neuropeptides, and promotes the formation of myelin by schwann cells as well [58].
2. Carotenoids, the lipid-soluble pigments, are light yellow to deep red in color found abundantly in plant tissue [58]. Lycopene, a type of carotenoid, which is best known for its potent antioxidant property, inhibits lipid peroxidation and enhances the activity of superoxide dismutase (SOD) [58].
3. Plant phenols are widely spread in purple-hued fruits and vegetables in particular [58].
4. Glutathione (GSH) is a potent thiol antioxidant, consisted of glutamate, cysteine and glycine amino acids [54]. GSH can be repaired by vitamin C [59].
5. Including SOD, glutathione peroxidase (GPx) and catalase (CAT) [58].
6. Retrieved from: https://www.hydroassoc.org/foods-to-nourish-the-brain/ and https://www.nm.org/healthbeat/healthy-tips/nutrition/best-food-for-a-healthy-brain

Blueberries, bursting with abundant antioxidants, are able to attenuate inflammation.

Leafy Greens, such as broccoli and spinach, are a rich source of vitamins and minerals.

Fruits, rich in vitamin C, protect the brain against cell damage, and may even prevent AD.

Walnuts, rich in omega-3s, polyunsaturated fats, polyphenols, antioxidants, and vitamin E, may help reduce oxidative damage and inflammation.

Fatty Fish, high in omega-3s, can help improve learning and memory.

Turmeric, a strong antioxidant with a potent anti-inflammatory impact, directly nourishes the brain by bypassing the blood-brain barrier.

Eggs are dense in healthy nutrients, a good source of choline, alleviating inflammation and promoting brain function, and are also rich in tryptophan, the precursor of serotonin.

Dark Chocolate is rich in antioxidants, which improve brain blood flow, prevent blood clots, and protect against cell damage.

Since the brain, as the chief organ, is accountable for regulating numerous biological processes within the body, in addition to its multitude of functions, maintaining its health and strength is critically important for achieving overall wellness and progressing toward flourishing. Lifestyle enrichment through incorporating fruitful habits, such as those mentioned in this chapter, into existing daily routines, can be a beneficial action in this regard. In addition, on the path to realizing full potential, paying attention to daily thoughts, as potent fuel for the mind, is also of considerable importance owing to their significant impacts not only on emotions and behaviors but also, ultimately, on the quality of life and future consequences. If we take a precise look at our thoughts, how constructive do we find them? Do they help us move forward or hold us back? Although making a change for the better, whether in lifestyle or mindset, can put us on the path toward prosperity, it does not always occur with ease, primarily due to external or internal obstacles. Besides, the identification and removal of these setbacks, which are like the stones in the river's path, is not often feasible on one's own, and here is exactly where another approach can be of assistance: Coaching, The New Technology for Change.[1] In this procedure, through applying essential skills including attentive listening and powerful questioning in addition to a variety of other competencies, in an empathetic, non-judgmental space, the coach helps the coachees attain greater awareness both about themselves and their issues. Indeed, coaching empowers clients to embark on an internal journey, where they can delve deeper into their inner selves, gain new insights, and apply them to overcome challenges. Since any clues for tackling the problem emerge from within the clients themselves, there is greater commitment and internal motivation to execute the defined actions. Actually, in coaching, clients discover their unique solution from within, through utilizing their strengths and creativity, rather than relying on external resources. Thus,

---
1. Ahmadi, I., et al. (2024). *Coaching Insights*. North Star Success.

coaching, as a novel approach of thinking, can serve people in a more profound understanding of themselves and their inner wealth, aiming to fulfill their full potential, since it firmly believes that clients are capable, creative, and resourceful, able to unravel their issues.

I greatly appreciate your valuable companionship. To bring this chapter to a close, I am really enthusiastic to know:

What insights did you acquire from reading this content?

And how would these insights assist you in achieving your utmost performance?

If you would like to connect with me for more discussions, **please use the address below:**
✉ amiraslanib@gmail.com
Good luck in your amazing journey of flourishing!

Banafsheh Amiraslani
Brain Health Coach and Flourishing Instructor

References:

1. Green, C. S., & Bavelier, D. (2008). Exercising your brain: A review of human brain plasticity and training-induced learning. *Psychology and Aging, 23*(4), 692–701.

2. Shors, T. J., Olson, R. L., Bates, M. E., Selby, E. A., & Alderman, B. L. (2014). Mental and Physical (MAP) Training: a neurogenesis-inspired intervention that enhances health in humans. *Neurobiology of Learning and Memory, 115*, 3–9.

3. Curlik, D. M. 2nd., & Shors, T. J. (2013). Training your brain: Do mental and physical (MAP) training enhance cognition through the process of neurogenesis in the hippocampus? *Neuropharmacology, 64*(1), 506–514.

4. Shors, T. J. (2014). The adult brain makes new neurons, and effortful learning keeps them alive. *Current Directions in Psychological Science, 23*(5), 311–318.

5. Shors, T. J., Anderson, M. L., Curlik, D. M. 2nd., & Nokia, M. S. (2012). Use it or lose it: How neurogenesis keeps the brain fit for learning. *Behavioural Brain Research, 227*(2), 450–458.

6. Deng, W., Aimone, J. B., & Gage, F. H. (2010). New neurons and new memories: how does adult hippocampal neurogenesis affect learning and memory? *Nature Reviews Neuroscience, 11*(5), 339–350.

7. Kempermann, G., Song, H., & Gage, F. H. (2015). Neurogenesis in the adult hippocampus. *Cold Spring Harbor Perspectives in Biology, 7*(9), a018812.

8. Bjork, R. A., Dunlosky, J., & Kornell, N. (2013). Self-regulated learning: beliefs, techniques, and illusions. *Annual Review of Psychology, 64*, 417–444.

9. May, A. (2011). Experience-dependent structural plasticity in the adult human brain. *Trends in Cognitive Sciences, 15*(10), 475–482.

10. Goldberg, H. (2022). Growing brains, nurturing minds-Neuroscience as an educational tool to support students' development as life-long

learners. *Brain Sciences*, *12*(12).

11. Fuchs, E., & Flügge, G. (2014). Adult neuroplasticity: more than 40 years of research. *Neural Plasticity*, *2014:2014:541870*.

12. Chen, S. H. A., & Goodwill, A. M. (2022). Neuroplasticity and adult learning. K. Evans et al. (eds.), *Third international handbook of lifelong learning*, Springer International Handbooks of Education, (pp. 1–19).

13. Malakasis, N., Chavlis, S., & Poirazi P. (2023). Synaptic turnover promotes efficient learning in bio-realistic spiking neural networks. *bioRxiv* [Preprint].

14. Guglielman, E. (2012). *The ageing brain: Neuroplasticity and lifelong learning*. eLearning Papers. 1-7.

15. Owens, M. T., & Tanner, K. D. (2017). Teaching as brain changing: Exploring connections between neuroscience and innovative teaching. *CBE—Life Sciences Education*, *16*(2):fe2.

16. Baumgart, M., Snyder, H. M., Carrillo, M. C., Fazio, S., Kim, H., & Johns, H. (2015). Summary of the evidence on modifiable risk factors for cognitive decline and dementia: A population-based perspective. *Alzheimer's & Dementia*, *11*(6), 718–726.

17. Howell, J. L., Koudenburg, N., Loschelder, D. D., Weston, D., Fransen, K., Dominicis, S. D., Gallagher, S., & Haslam, S. A. (2014). Happy but unhealthy: The relationship between social ties and health in an emerging network. *European Journal of Social Psychology*, *44*(6), 612–621.

18. McEwen, B. S. (2017). Neurobiological and systemic effects of chronic stress, 1, 2470547017692328.

19. Kim, E. J., & Kim, J. J. (2023). Neurocognitive effects of stress: a metaparadigm perspective. *Molecular Psychiatry*, *28*(7), 2750–2763.

20. Kim, B.-K., Ko, I.-G., Kim, S.-E., Kim, C.-J., Yoon, J.-S., Baik, H.-H., Jin, B.-K., Lee, C.-Y., Baek, S.-B., & Shin, M.-S. (2013). Impact of several types of stresses on short-term memory and apoptosis in the hippocampus of rats. *International Neurourology Journal*, 17(3),

114–120.

21. Flexman, R. (2021). Lifelong learning: A key weapon in Delaware's fight against cognitive decline. *Delaware Journal of Public Health*, *7*(4), 124–127.

22. Martino, J., Pegg, J., & Frates, E. P. (2015). The connection prescription: Using the power of social interactions and the deep desire for connectedness to empower health and wellness. *American Journal of Lifestyle Medicine*, *11*(6), 466–475.

23. Fredrickson, B. L. (2004). The broaden-and-build theory of positive emotions. *Philosophical Transactions of the Royal Society of London. Series B, Biological Sciences*, *359*(1449), 1367–1378.

24. Fredrickson, B. L. (2001). The role of positive emotions in positive psychology. The broaden-and-build theory of positive emotions. *American Psychologist*, *56*(3), 218–226.

25. Niemann, L., Gruner, C. v., Zhang, X. C., Margraf, J., & Totzeck, C. (2023). Positive emotions training (PoET) as an online intervention to improve mental health: a feasibility study. *BMC Public Health*, *23*(1).

26. Yin, J. (2019). Study on the progress of neural mechanism of positive emotions. *Translational Neuroscience*, *10*, 93–98.

27. Fredrickson, B. L., & Branigan, C. (2005). Positive emotions broaden the scope of attention and thought-action repertoires. *Cognition and Emotion*, *19*(3), 313–332.

28. Huppert, F. A. (2009). Psychological well-being: Evidence regarding its causes and consequences. *Applied Psychology: Health and Well-Being*, *1*(2), 137–164.

29. Hanlon, C. A., Dowdle, L. T., & Jones, J. (2016). Biomarkers for success: Using neuroimaging to predict relapse and develop brain stimulation treatments for cocaine dependent individuals. *International Review of Neurobiology*, *129*, 125–156.

30. Olguín, H. J., Guzmán, D. C., García, E. H., & Mejía, G. B. (2015). The role of dopamine and its dysfunction as a consequence of oxidative

stress. *Oxidative Medicine and Cellular Longevity*, 2016:2016:9730467.

31. Dfarhud, D., Malmir, M., & Khanahmadi, M. (2014). Happiness & health: The biological factors- Systematic review article. *Iranian Journal of Public Health*, *43*(11), 1468–1477.

32. Martins, F. H., & Cuesta, S. (2021). *Citrobacter rodentium* infection at the gut-brain axis interface. *Current Opinion in Microbiology*, *63*, 59–65.

33. Young, S. N. (2007). How to increase serotonin in the human brain without drugs. *Journal of Psychiatry and Neuroscience*, *32*(6), 394–399.

34. Guidozzi, F., Guidozzi, D., & Guidozzi, Y. (2025). Neuro-anatomy and neuro-physiology of happiness in ageing women. *EGO European Gynecology and Obstetrics*, *7*(1), 43–47.

35. Blum, K., Baron, D., McLaughlin, T., & Gold, M. S. (2020). Molecular neurological correlates of endorphinergic/dopaminergic mechanisms in reward circuitry linked to endorphinergic deficiency syndrome (EDS). *Journal of the Neurological Sciences*, *411*.

36. Tracy, L. M., Georgiou-Karistianis, N., Gibson, S. J., & Giummarra, M. J. (2015). Oxytocin and the modulation of pain experience: Implications for chronic pain management. *Neuroscience & Biobehavioral Reviews*, *55*, 53–67.

37. Jimenez, M. P., Deville, N. V., Elliott, E. G., Schiff, J. E., Wilt, G. E., Hart, J. E., & James, P. (2021). Associations between nature exposure and health: A review of the evidence. *International Journal of Environmental Research and Public Health*, 18(9):4790.

38. Bratman, G. N., Anderson, C. B., Berman, M. G., Cochran, B., de Vries, S., Flanders, J., Folke, C., Frumkin, H., Gross, J. J., Hartig, T., Kahn, P. H. J. r., Kuo, M., Lawler, J. J., Levin, P. S., Lindahl, T., Meyer-Lindenberg, A., Mitchell, R., Ouyang, Z., Roe, J., Scarlett, L., Smith, J. R., van den Bosch, M., Wheeler, B. W., White, M. P., Zheng, H., Daily, G. C. (2019). Nature and mental health: An ecosystem service perspective. *Science Advances*, 5(7):caax0903.

39. Capaldi, C. A., Dopko, R. L., & Zelenski, J. M. (2014). The relationship between nature connectedness and happiness: a meta-analysis. *Frontiers in Psychology, 5:976.*

40. Guardini, B., Secco, L., Moè, A., Pazzaglia, F., De Mas, G., Vegetti, M., Perrone, R., Tilman, A., Renzi, M., & Rapisarda, S. (2023). A three-day forest-bathing retreat enhances positive affect, vitality, optimism, and gratitude: An option for green-care tourism in Italy? *Forests, 14*(7):1423.

41. Lengieza, M. L., Richardson, M., & Aviste, R. (2025). Situation networks: The emotions and activities that are central to nature-connectedness experiences. *Journal of Environmental Psychology, 101.*

42. Grassini, S., Segurini, G. V., & Koivisto, M. (2022). Watching nature videos promotes physiological restoration: Evidence from the modulation of alpha waves in electroencephalography. *Frontiers in Psychology,* 13:871143.

43. Krishnakumar, D., Hamblin, M. R., & Lakshmanan, S. (2015). Meditation and yoga can modulate brain mechanisms that affect behavior and anxiety-A modern scientific perspective. *Ancient Science, 2*(1), 13–19.

44. Jamil, A., Gutlapalli, S. D., Ali, M., Oble, M. J. P., Sonia, S. N., George, S., Shahi, S. R., Ali, Z., Abaza, A., Mohammed, L. (2023). Meditation and its mental and physical health benefits in 2023. *Cureus, 15*(6):e40650.

45. Dobrakowski, P., Blaszkiewicz, M., & Skalski, S. (2020). Changes in the electrical activity of the brain in the alpha and theta bands during prayer and meditation. *International Journal of Environmental Research and Public Health,* 17(24):9567.

46. Lorenzo, A. D., Lattke, L. S., & Rabaglietti, E. (2023). Creativity and resilience: a mini-review on post-pandemic resources for adolescents and young adults. *Frontiers in Public Health, 11*:1117539.

47. Crick, R., McDermott, T., & Hutchison, N. (2021). Learning design for sustainable development. *Journal of Education, Teaching and Social Studies, 3*(3).

48. Hossain, M. N., Lee, J., Choi, H., Kwak, Y.-S., & Kim, J. (2024). The impact of exercise on depression: how moving makes your brain and

body feel better. *Physical Activity and Nutrition, 28*(2), 43–51.

49. Basso, J. C., & Suzuki, W. A. (2017). The effects of acute exercise on mood, cognition, neurophysiology, and neurochemical pathways: A review. *Brain Plasticity, 2*(2), 127–152.

50. Datu, J. A. D., Valdez, J. P. M., McInerney, D. M., & Cayubit, R. F. (2022). The effects of gratitude and kindness on life satisfaction, positive emotions, negative emotions, and COVID-19 anxiety: An online pilot experimental study. *Applied Psychology: Health and Well-Being, 14*(2), 347–361.

51. Eugene, A. R., & Masiak, J. (2015). The neuroprotective aspects of sleep. *MEDtube Science, 3*(1), 35–40.

52. Hauglund, N. L., Pavan, C., & Nedergaard, M. (2020). Cleaning the sleeping brain – the potential restorative function of the glymphatic system. *Current Opinion in Physiology, 15*, 1–6.

53. Lee, J. G., Woo, Y. S., Park, S. W., Seog, D.-H., Seo, M. K., & Bahk, W.-M. (2019). The neuroprotective effects of melatonin: Possible role in the pathophysiology of neuropsychiatric disease. *Brain Sciences, 9*(10), 285.

54. Aslani, B. A., & Ghobadi, S. (2016). Studies on oxidants and antioxidants with a brief glance at their relevance to the immune system. *Life Sciences, 146*, 163–173.

55. Muscaritoli, M. (2021). The impact of nutrients on mental health and well-being: Insights from the literature. *Frontiers in Nutrition, 8:*656290.

56. Muscolo, A., Mariateresa, O., Giulio, T., Mariateresa, R. (2024). Oxidative stress: The role of antioxidant phytochemicals in the prevention and treatment of diseases. *International Journal of Molecular Sciences, 25*(6):3264.

57. Lalkovičová, M., & Danielisová, V. (2016). Neuroprotection and antioxidants. *Neural Regeneration Research, 11*(6), 865–874.

58. Guest, J. A., & Grant, R. S. (2012). Effects of dietary derived

antioxidants on the central nervous system. *International Journal of Nutrition, Pharmacology, Neurological Diseases, 2*(3), 185–197.

59. Lee, K. H., Cha, M., & Lee, B. H. (2020). Neuroprotective effect of antioxidants in the brain. *International Journal of Molecular Sciences, 21*(19):7152.

60. Poulose, S. M., Miller, M. G., Scott, T., & Shukitt-Hale, B. (2017). Nutritional factors affecting adult neurogenesis and cognitive function. *Advances in Nutrition, 8*(6), 804–811.

61. Freeman, L. R., & Keller, J. N. (2012). Oxidative stress and cerebral endothelial cells: Regulation of the blood-brain-barrier and antioxidant based interventions. *Biochimica et Biophysica Acta, 1822*(5), 822–829.

62. Beltz, B. S., Tlusty, M. F., Benton, J. L., & Sandeman, D. C. (2007). Omega-3 fatty acids upregulate adult neurogenesis. *Neuroscience Letters, 415*(2), 154–158.

63. Perrone, S., Tataranno, L. M., Stazzoni, G., Ramenghi, L., & Buonocore, G. (2015). Brain susceptibility to oxidative stress in the perinatal period. *Journal of Maternal-Fetal & Neonatal Medicine, 28 Suppl 1:2291-5.*

But Why Now?
Rebuilding the Wheel of Life for Growth and Flourishing

Dr. Mostafa Azimi

But Why Now?
Rebuilding the Wheel of Life for Growth and Flourishing

Dr. Mostafa Azimi

Attorney at Law and Legal Consultant, Doctor in Business Administration, High-Performance Master Trainer

In the Hospital, Amidst Questions and Silences

The doorbell woke us both. "It's 2:47 AM! Who could it be at this hour?!" I panicked and rushed to the intercom. It was Maryam, my friend Reza's wife. "Come on up," I said, instructing my wife to guide her while I quickly dressed. We waited at the apartment door. When she emerged from the elevator, she exclaimed, "Why aren't you answering your phones?!" We ushered her inside. She continued, "I've been calling for 25 minutes, and neither of you answered. I thought I'd die before I got here." My wife responded, "You know our routine; our landline isn't connected, and our cell phones go silent after 10 PM. We go to bed by 10:30 PM." Realizing this, she lowered her head and said, "I'm so sorry, I completely forgot. Honestly, I'm very agitated. Reza is in the hospital. He had an accident; a car hit him. The emergency room called me, and Saman wasn't home, so I wanted to ask for your help."

I got ready quickly and we set off. I parked near the hospital and hurried to the emergency room. Maryam had arrived earlier and was speaking with a nurse. "What's happening?" I asked. She replied, "No specific news yet." We found two empty chairs and sat down to wait. After a few minutes of silence, Maryam said, "Please, Mostafa, I apologize again for how I spoke about the phones. What seems normal in your life has no meaning in our lives. I used to be glad my husband is a lawyer, but that was foolish! He leaves at 6 AM, and by 11 PM, I call him asking where he is, and he says he'll be home in half an hour! And if he is home, he is either on a call or someone is calling him!"

"That's one of the problems with being a lawyer: some people are inconsiderate and call on holidays or outside of working hours."

"Well, they can call, but can't Reza just say it's outside of working hours?! Someone calls at midnight saying it's an emergency, and in the end, we find out it's something for next month!"

"What can I say? I get those calls too, but not at midnight."

"Clearly, when you have a set bedtime and don't give your home number for work, you shouldn't have these problems."

"You're just upsetting yourself more with these thoughts. Hopefully, everything will be fine."

The nurse arrived, handed me Reza's prescription, and instructed us to get his medications immediately. Maryam took the prescription and said, "I'll get them. Please stay here." As she folded it, she sighed, "Yes, Mostafa, I also thought everything would be fine."

A Court Between Us, Without a Judge

I was in the waiting room when a patient's companion insisted on staying by their severely ill loved one. The guard took his arm and guided him toward the waiting area. This scene reminded me of a year ago, when Reza and I last saw each other. It was a Wednesday evening, and we had an appointment at Reza's office. It was the end of the month, time to wrap up our work. We were busy when the office bell rang. The secretary opened the door. It was one of our clients. Without coordination, he asked the secretary for Reza and, ignoring her warning that "they're in a meeting," entered the room. He declined my invitation to sit and said, "What kind of verdict is this that you got for me after a year?!" Reza said, "We're working on the appeal."

"My life is in ruins, and you're so relaxed?"

Reza replied aggressively, "What are we supposed to do, hang ourselves? The verdict has been issued, and we must object." He raised his voice, "Stop! Objections. How do you know it won't be the same again?" Reza replied, "Sir, be considerate! It's not up to us; the judge issues the verdict." The client looked at me and said, "Weren't you the one who told me not to worry?"

Taken aback, I responded, "I told you that?!" The client replied, "No, not you; it was him. But what's the difference?"

BUT WHY NOW?

I fell silent. He asked, "What happened? You're quiet." Reza added, "Speak properly; this is a workplace."

"I'll show you what speaking properly means!" The client said before leaving the room.

A deadly silence filled the room, charged with anger. Who was angry at whom? Reza at the client, me at the client, Reza at me, or me at Reza? Reza asked, "Mostafa, why did you say that?"

"What?"

"The way you turned to him and said, 'Did I tell you not to worry?'"

"Of course! If I didn't say it, why accept it?"

"Let's say I did; it was a joint case, and the responsibility for its failure is on both of us."

This had long been a problem in my relationship with Reza. I had addressed it several times, but he wasn't listening. I took the chance to say my piece one last time. I said, "Yes, when two people take on a case, the responsibility is joint, but the issue now isn't losing the case; it's work ethics." He said sarcastically, "Please enlighten us." Ignoring him, I continued, "I've read clients' documents and told you the chances of success were low, yet you enthusiastically promised and persuaded them to sign. In the end, the client lost." He asked, "Which case?"

"Mr. Hosseini's or Mr. Taghizadeh's. And sometimes, after

reviewing the case, I realized the client was clearly right. However, in the meeting, you discussed the difficulty of winning and the weakness of the documents in a way that dashed the client's hopes—and mine too. After you crushed their hopes, you told him, 'But you've come to the right place. If we are your lawyers, you'll see what kind of verdict we get.'

"I was the lawyer for those cases. They have nothing to do with you!"

"Yes, they're unrelated now, but these were our joint cases that I refused to take on because of your behavior."

"You saw the verdict I got in Mr. Taghizadeh's case! So I should be blamed for winning?"

"You know what I mean; don't play dumb. We're discussing ethics, both professional and human. My point is, why give false promises to a client who has lost part of their life, forcing them to spend more on court and lawyer fees? When everything points to a win for the client, why discourage them to secure a better contract, so you can later take credit for a verdict that would've gone in their favor anyway?"

Reza, growing angrier, said, "If you don't know how to work, please don't preach."

"You think I don't know how to work?! That money you're earning—it's not right. You've built your comfort on the backs of others."

This made him furious, and with trembling hands, he said,

"Come here for a second." He dragged me to the office exit, opened the door, and said, "Mr. Righteous! Please go to your own office and take on cases where the bread is earned honestly! When I die, don't come to my grave to pray for my soul, because I want to go to hell!" He then politely escorted me out and slammed the door.

From Silence to Outcry

Reza had been irritable for some time, but I never expected this behavior from him. I was shocked, standing in front of the elevator, thinking that Reza would come to apologize any minute. Then Saman's voice brought me back to reality. "Hi, Uncle, are you okay?" he asked. "Hi, dear. Yes, why do you ask?"

"I called you several times; didn't you hear me?"

"My thoughts are preoccupied."

"Where's Dad? What happened? I saw Mom's message telling me to get here, but she's not answering."

"Calm down. Dad had a small accident; he's still in the emergency room."

Tears streamed down Saman's face. I comforted him when Maryam arrived, yelling at Saman, "Where have you been? I called you 50 times!" Saman replied, "Mom, you know how I felt last night. I told you I was going to my friend's. My phone died." I said, "Leave it now. Thank God Saman is here."

Saman stood up, walked a few steps away, leaned against a pillar, and closed his eyes. I told Maryam, "Don't be too hard on Saman."

"Oh God, I can't help it. Poor Saman, I don't know how he spent last night."

Saman asked, "Mom, why isn't anyone here? Not my uncles or aunts..."

"Son, I didn't tell anyone. It happened so suddenly. I only asked Mostafa for help."

"Yeah, right, Mom. Just say none of them showed up—why would they?"

"Stop it, Saman!"

Saman said with a bitter smile, "Surely if Dad were here, he would say: 'My son, these two-faced people are like flies around honey. They only stick around when they smell money.'" He turned to me and continued, "You know my dad sees everything through the lens of money; respect, life, family, happiness—all pass through that filter."

I said, "Saman, do you think it's right to talk about your dad like this in front of others?"

"Am I lying? I remember two years ago, the landlord threw my aunt's belongings onto the street. Dad didn't bat an eye. Mom suggested helping them rent a place, and he said, 'Do you think that good-for-nothing son-in-law will pay me back?' In the end, they stayed at Uncle Mohsen's for 40 days.

Why don't you mention Uncle Mohsen? Five years ago, when someone was trying to seize their house, he asked Dad for help, and Dad said, 'Go complain to the police; they'll make his life hell.' No matter how much Mom urged him to help, he insisted, 'I'm not the family lawyer; he should hire one; this isn't my work!' Uncle Mostafa, I remember you solving his problem. Or poor Uncle Peyman, who asked to work in Dad's office but was turned down. With a bachelor's degree, he ended up in a lumber mill, and early in his youth, two of his fingers went under the saw. Which story should I tell? Do you remember Aunt Leila...?"

Maryam said, "Saman, that's enough!" He replied, "Okay, I'll stop." With an agitated expression, he continued slowly, "But please, don't say you didn't call them; say you called, and none came; they didn't want to come." With a lump in his throat, he sat two rows behind us and buried his head in his hands. Maryam said sadly, "If only I had just one sorrow to bear, it would be a blessing."

The Turning Point

Reza was better and had been moved to a ward. I went to his bedside and greeted him. He turned his head and looked at me in surprise. I moved closer, placed my hand on his forehead, and asked how he was. He weakly replied, "I'm fine." I said, "You'll get better." Given his condition, we exchanged brief pleasantries. He asked, "So where's Saman?"

Saman had calmed down a bit when he heard his father was

better, but he still hadn't agreed to see him. Reza, sensing this, sighed and said, "He has every right not to come." Then he looked directly into my eyes and said, "I lost everything." I replied, "Everything will be alright. Just focus on your health for now." He spoke haltingly, "Health? Stomach ulcers, stress, heart problems… What's left of my health? This is where I'm at now—I don't even know if any part of me is still okay."

"Thank God it turned out alright; just calm down."

"I can't calm down; do you know why Saman hasn't come to see me or why I'm here? Last night, I got home at midnight. No one was home. Half an hour later, they arrived. I asked where they'd been, and Saman said, 'Dad, didn't you know we were supposed to go for my proposal[1] today?' I just realized what a mess I'd made and said, 'Why didn't you remind me?' Maryam got angry and said, 'We told you the night before! Check your phone; see how many times I called you today and you didn't answer. I sent you texts; you didn't even see those.' I said, 'You went, thank God, congratulations!' As soon as I said that, Saman went into his room and slammed the door. Maryam sneered, 'Congratulations on what? Because you didn't come, we were left in a predicament. However we tried to explain that an important meeting came up for you, they said, "A meeting more important than their son's proposal?" In the end, they said, "Please allow us to think it over, and if

---

1. *khastegāri* is a traditional Iranian ritual in which a prospective groom, often accompanied by his family, formally visits the bride's family to express his interest in marriage and propose. It typically involves discussions about compatibility, family expectations, and future plans.

our answer is positive, we will inform you." Of course, from the way they said "if," the answer was clear.' Last night, for the first time, I felt sorry for my son. I felt terrible. I went out for a walk. On the street, I couldn't hear the cars. My mind was busy with Maryam and Saman's words. I crossed the street to buy cigarettes, and then I don't know what happened."

"Don't worry, You'll be better. You'll take your family and go for Saman's proposal again."

Reza, shedding tears, said, "I didn't realize when this child grew up. I'm very worried about him."

"I'll find him and bring him to you. You just rest."

Reza squeezed my hand, looked into my eyes, and said, "I apologize for my behavior."

I felt as if I had been waiting a year to hear that. I smiled and said, "Forget about it, my friend." Reza mentioned that when he was discharged, he would change everything when Maryam arrived. I said, "You came just at the right time. Reza's completely changed since the accident; come see what he's saying!" Reza, with a faint smile, promised to make up for the past. Maryam exclaimed, "Has your brain been scrambled, Reza?! You've never said anything like this!" Then, as if rejuvenated, she took Reza's hand and placed her other hand on his forehead. I said, "Alright, I'll leave you and go find Saman."

Seize the Moment

It took me half an hour to convince Saman over the phone to see his father. Everything seemed to be going well. I collapsed onto a bench in the hospital courtyard and closed my eyes, waiting for Saman to arrive. Exhausted, I fell asleep. Suddenly, I was startled awake by a scream. "Is that Maryam crying? Did she say Reza?" Anxiety overwhelmed me. I rushed toward the ward. I couldn't believe it. Reza had a heart attack! His promises from forty minutes ago, Maryam's smile, Saman's decision to reconcile... I was in shock.[1] In that moment, I understood how quickly it can get too late.[2]

Returning to Balance, Returning to Life

In life's twists and turns, we often cling to one aspect and forget others. Work, success, money, or family can absorb us so much that we lose relationships, health, or inner peace. Reza's story reflects this imbalance. Perhaps if he had considered his **Wheel of Life** sooner, he would have realized that life is more than just courtrooms and contracts.

The Wheel of Life reminds us that to live a healthy and meaningful life, we must balance various dimensions, including work, family, friends, personal growth, health, recreation, and spirituality. Sometimes it's enough to pause

---

1. This story is not real; it is a fictional narrative combining various experiences written by the author with the aim of reflecting on life balance, professional ethics, and human relationships.
2. A poem by Gheisar Aminpour, a noted Iranian poet, that reminds us of how swiftly time passes and how unexpectedly opportunities can be lost.

and see which parts of this wheel are unbalanced, then consciously decide to fill them.

No one wants a day to come when others say, "He was very successful, but..." A balanced life is the only way to address those "buts."

But Why Now?
Rebuilding the Wheel of Life for Growth and Flourishing

About the Author

Dr. Mostafa Azimi is a legal consultant with

a Master's degree in law, an attorney-at-law with over 28 years of experience, and a member of the Tehran Bar Association. He also holds a Doctorate in Business Administration (DBA) from the University of Tehran.

Mostafa holds the profession of law in high regard. When asked, "Do you say law is the best profession just because you're a lawyer?" he replies, "No — I became a lawyer because law is the best profession." For Mostafa, law is not just a legal practice; it is an interdisciplinary endeavor. A great lawyer, he believes, should be well-versed in literature, art, sociology, management, and psychology. Each case he handles presents ethical, social, and psychological complexities.

While Mostafa is passionate about law, teaching holds a special place in his heart. He considers teaching a calling and believes the best way to learn is to teach. Over the past 12 years, he has taught hundreds of students in law and banking, transforming complex legal concepts into accessible ideas through his engaging style.

Building on his extensive experience, Mostafa recently completed the Professional Trainer Development Program in Personal and Organizational Flourishing at the North Star Coaching and Training Academy in Canada. This ICF-accredited training allowed him to create a unique educational experience—formed through 34 years of personal development studies, 28 years of legal practice, and 12 years of teaching—benefiting the people of Iran, especially fellow attorneys.

His wife often says that when Mostafa starts writing, the pen dances in his hand. His writings can elicit laughter with their wit and move readers to tears with their depth. Don't believe it? Just ask the many readers who have shared heartfelt feedback (and yes—he welcomes yours too!).[1]

When asked why he writes, Mostafa often refers to a quote by motivational speaker Les Brown, who describes the graveyard as the richest place on earth—where countless unfulfilled

---

1. Please check his Instagram account: mostafaazimi.me and see the highlight about the feedbacks.

dreams and unwritten books lie buried. And so, he writes—before it's too late.

After reviewing an early draft of this chapter, someone asked him, "Did your late friend's family give you permission to publish their story?" The question thrilled and worried him—thrilled that the story felt authentic and worried that others might mistake it for real.

Mostafa has mastered the art of blending seriousness with humor. Your job as the reader? To discern when he's serious—and when he's not.

So, if you're about to connect with him, click gently.[1]

https://thecartino.ir/c/7215352

---

1. A contemporary adaptation of Sohrab Sepehri's poem *The Sound of Water's Footsteps*. Here, the word *click* replaces *come*, blending poetic tone with modern digital language.

From Foreign Lands to Inner Truth
A Journey Toward Flourishing:
From Immigration to Identity Restoration in an Unstable World

Negar Dianat

From Foreign Lands to Inner Truth
A Journey Toward Flourishing:
From Immigration to Identity Restoration in an Unstable World

Negar Dianat
Health and Flourishing Coach and Consultant

You are walking down a road when you encounter a madman shouting, "Run! Run! Your house is on fire!" Despite knowing he is insane, you rush toward your home to ensure the safety of your family. The brain is like this madman; it often plays tricks on your mind. Again and again, you find yourself running, feeling anxious, and falling for the deceptions of your own mind.

Anxiety was an inseparable part of my life. There is an old belief that pain and suffering carry a message that repeats until we understand it. Physical and mental alarms go off repeatedly until we review our lives. This happened to me in late summer or early fall of 2022. It was either September or early October; during the pleasant weather in Canada, with my parents in Montreal, I struggled to enjoy life. I was grappling with the problems in Iran, and my jumbled thoughts left me paralyzed and unable to take action.

Amidst these thoughts and worries, the beep of the heart monitor and a sudden pain in my left arm jolted me awake. A red light circled my head, and I passed out. I woke up in an ambulance on the way to the hospital, an ambulance that was not sounding its siren. I thought to myself, "How casually Canadian emergencies handle everything!" The nurse checked my blood pressure, and when I asked, "Why aren't we reaching the hospital?" she calmly replied, "Don't worry, we'll get there." Then she asked, "Why didn't you go out and walk when you saw your blood pressure was high?" I assumed she was joking. How could I walk with a blood pressure of twenty over twelve? The nurse said, "If you had gone out and walked, your brain would have been activated, your stress would have decreased, and your blood pressure would have returned to normal. You're just anxious, that's all!"

I had heard this before: "You're just anxious!" I was having a stroke, my left arm was aching, and this nurse simply told me to go for a walk! We arrived at the hospital, and the check-up process began. They attached the ECG device electrodes to my body. I decided to let go of everything, but I knew this was just talk. I started to reflect on my life's journey.

Immigration: A Journey to a New World

To narrate this story, I must return to the hot summer of 2014. We had just celebrated our fifteenth wedding anniversary and completed a three-year process to obtain a visa. It was time for my husband, our ten-year-old child, and me to immigrate to Canada. At that time, I didn't realize that immigrating meant more than just leaving; it required erasing parts of my memory. I thought we were merely changing our residence, but in reality, our identities were shifting. The man I had lived with for fifteen years had dimensions I had never seen, and I found myself exploring the darker aspects of my own existence. I had no idea how profoundly immigration would alter my identity and mindset.

We rented two rooms in the house of a respectable Iranian lady and spent a strange week there—a temporary stay with someone who was familiar and yet a stranger! Inside the house, everything was like Iran, but the windows opened to a different world. Outside, we were bewildered, dealing with paperwork and administrative forms.

From opening a bank account to registering my daughter for school, everything was different from what we knew in Iran. The laws, social behaviors, and even daily tasks such as shopping and using public transportation were new to us. In a world that felt pre-planned and formal, I had to learn to rebuild my life from scratch, much like a child unfamiliar with the adult world. Coming from an entirely Middle Eastern and almost patriarchal culture, I found myself in a setting where men and women worked side by side to build an equal world; a world where women were valued as much as men. But did this newfound equality and freedom mean my life was becoming easier? Not exactly. I was beginning to realize that the real challenge of immigration lay in changing myself.

Children adapt more easily to a new country. After six months, I was thrilled to see my daughter speaking French as if it were her mother tongue and thriving at school. However, I was so engrossed in my efforts that I didn't know how to enjoy this happiness. After much hard work, I found a job, gained Canadian experience, and finally reached my ideal position. Just when I thought I had stabilized, a letter arrived: "Your services are no longer needed."

At that moment, it felt like the world had collapsed on me. I thought I had reached the end of the line, but I didn't know that every end hides a new beginning. A while later, I found a better job in a calmer environment. This experience taught me one important lesson: "If you don't know how to face crises, the world will knock you down over and over again." I fell down many times until I understood the reasons for my failures.

Immigrant Woman: Multiple Roles and Loneliness in a New World

This was just the beginning of the real challenges. Being an immigrant woman meant not only coping with cultural differences but also navigating an unwanted journey into new roles and invisible pressures—a journey where you always had to stay strong, even when you were falling apart inside. After living with certain standards for thirty-nine years, you suddenly find yourself in a world where you must start from scratch. Should you lower your standards? No, you should maintain them, or even raise them. Yet, something inevitably changes. In your homeland, there was always someone by your side to help with chores or fill your lonely moments. Here, in this new land, everything depends on you; you shop, cook, wash, clean, and most importantly, you become lonely. You realize that loneliness is not just the absence of others, but the confrontation with your true self.

It's scary, isn't it? I believe it is. After all these years, it still feels that way. Perhaps this is where many immigrant women struggle. Here, caught between the traditions that shape you and the modernity that pressures you, there is an expectation to be both a traditional woman and an independent one—to work, manage the household, be a mother, and embody the modern woman that others look up to as a role model. But where in these roles is there room for yourself? These stresses, feelings of being ignored, and silent pressures accumulate gradually and lead to an unpleasant outcome known as *anxiety*!

The Shadow of Anxiety in a Foreign Land

Gradually, I had become accustomed to my circumstances, yet a part of my mind remained anxious. Although life was going well, it felt as though there was a void somewhere, one that my mind only amplified. It was the fall of 2019, five years after my immigration, when I experienced a panic attack for the first time. I had woken up in the middle of the night and couldn't fall back asleep. The only idea that came to me was to distract myself with my mobile phone. Suddenly, while scrolling through the news, I noticed the Iranian government's decision to filter the internet and launch a national intranet. In an instant, my mind began to scream: "I'm not going to see my family anymore. I'll never see Iran again." My thoughts repeated incessantly: "Forget Iran!" I felt my chest tighten and sweat bead on my face. I couldn't breathe. "I must be having a stroke," I thought. I rushed to the balcony to get some fresh air and took a few deep breaths. I wanted to wake a family member and call emergency services, but I began to feel better. I wasn't having a stroke; this was my first experience of a panic attack.

With the onset of the COVID-19 pandemic, my worries intensified, and I completely forgot about my previous panic attack. We were all homebound, consumed by news of vaccine production, washing and disinfecting, and experimenting with various recipes. Canada's exhausting winter, combined with home confinement, social distancing, remote work, and travel restrictions, multiplied our loneliness and anxiety. The events we all experienced contributed to a buildup of stress that many of us may not have fully realized. Thus, two years passed in this manner.

The second panic attack was much more severe and did not last just a few seconds; I experienced about five or six consecutive attacks within an hour. I called 911.[1] The emergency personnel arrived, but that night was filled only with pain, and even recalling it causes the pain to resurface. I wanted to cry, but I couldn't. The prescription was to rest and remain calm, but my problem was not physical; something deep within my soul felt injured.

---

1. The emergency phone number in Canada used in all situations where emergency, police, or firefighters are need.

My parents had come to Canada and were supposed to stay in Ottawa with my uncle's family for a week. On the way from Montreal to Ottawa, I suddenly felt short of breath and had a lump in my throat, as though a hand were squeezing it. Cold sweat rolled down my face as I worried about my parents. I took the nearest exit, and we sat in a McDonald's, eating French fries. I pretended everything was under control, but it wasn't. When we arrived at my uncle's house, I checked my blood pressure with a monitor and called an ambulance. I eventually felt better; it seemed to be a fleeting moment, and it was over.

After the Storm

The moment I lay on the hospital bed, the beeping of the heart monitor ringing in my ears, my entire ten-year journey since immigration unfolded behind my closed eyes, like a movie playing on a cinema screen—one sequence after another. After all the tests and examinations, it became clear that I had no heart problems; my only issue was chronic anxiety and stress. The doctor suggested that I speak with a family doctor and a counselor. My body had warned me many times, and now I understood that I needed to take those warnings seriously. These pressures were not just simple nervous pressures. Hearing that my problems stemmed from stress and anxiety left me more confused. Did that mean all those years of pressure and effort had culminated in this—just one label: chronic anxiety? This was not what I expected, but part of me knew that this diagnosis was the yellow light I had been ignoring for a long time. Perhaps it was a warning from within, signaling that it was time to change my path.

Although I had been speaking with my psychotherapist for a while, I had not attended psychotherapy sessions regularly. As soon as I felt better, I would skip the sessions. Then, after lengthy discussions and necessary check-ups, the family doctor diagnosed me with "grade two chronic anxiety" and insisted that I would not be able to return to a normal state without medication. Thus began my counseling sessions, alongside medication. From the very start, I was cautioned to be careful for a month until the medication gradually took effect. I improved, but not completely. A part of me remained stuck in old patterns, clinging to the backpack of anxiety and pain I had been carrying. Letting go of this backpack proved harder than I had imagined. It felt as if this pain kept my old self alive somewhere within me. It was at this point that I realized I needed something more than just relief from stress. I was searching for something akin to true peace.

A Journey Toward Peace

I knew there had to be another way. Psychotherapy and medication were not the only options, but I didn't know what that alternative path was or where to find it. One day, while browsing social networks, I came across one of Dr. Shahab Anari's posts: a short video discussing blooming, growth, self-awareness, and the principles of positive psychology. Until then, I had never heard of positive psychology. For me, like many others, psychology meant therapy and solving mental problems. I began extensive research and quickly immersed myself in the fascinating world of positive psychology and Dr. Martin Seligman's work. I made my decision; I had to pursue this path. I felt that the cure for my pain was right here, and indeed it was. I registered in the High-Performance Master Trainer Course at North Star Training and Coaching Academy to become a positive psychology practitioner. I learned about levels of awareness, self-love, stress management, time management, purposefulness, goal setting, and many other branches of this field. Now, I take a step forward every day and have changed significantly. The phrase "the savior is in the mirror" became my guiding light. Now, when I look in the mirror, I see a new self who has come a long way.

Given my professional background in the nutrition and food industries, and recognizing how changing my daily diet had positively impacted my condition, I decided to merge the paths of healthy nutrition and personal growth to help others. Through my studies in positive psychology, levels of awareness, and self-knowledge, a new world opened up to me. I stumbled many times but got back up, growing stronger with each setback. Although I lacked external support, I became my own advocate. Today, when I look back, I feel proud of myself. I firmly pat my shoulder and say: "Well done! You have come a long way, and now you are ready to help others make their journey easier."

We should remember that immigration is not just a change

of residence; it is a redefinition of oneself. You are not alone in this experience, just as I was not. Many people around the globe face numerous challenges. While we may not have a place in others' struggles, we hear their stories and learn from them. Each story serves as a light that illuminates a path for us, and if we follow this path to the end, perhaps one day our story will become a light for someone else.

Now, years after the start of this winding journey, filled with anxieties, longings, failures, and midnight awakenings, I have come to a simple truth: not everything is meant to be under control. I am not always expected to be strong or to shine. What truly matters is the ability to rise after every fall, to honestly reflect on oneself, and to learn from every crisis. Anxiety is still part of my life, but it no longer controls my life. Now, I am a woman who has taken root in the midst of storms; not despite the hardships, but because of them! My house may have burned down, but in the ruins, I have discovered my true self, which means flourishing even in an uncertain and unstable world.

Today, after years of navigating the storms of immigration, anxiety, loneliness, and change, I have realized that flourishing means standing among instability and consciously choosing a life path. I have learned that home is not just a place, but a feeling that you create within yourself. My identity is no longer tied to geography or imposed roles; rather, it is based on awareness, acceptance, and love for myself. This journey of coming back to yourself, is not a one-time trip but a continuous road of self-recognition in the mirror of experiences and life choices. There are still moments when my mind screams, but now I know I can hear its voice, respond empathetically, and choose a brighter path.

From Foreign Lands to Inner Truth

A Journey Toward Flourishing: From Immigration to Identity Restoration in an Unstable World

About the Author

Negar Dianat is a certified health and wellness coach and consultant who helps individuals achieve a healthier lifestyle and manage stress to create physical and mental balance. Combining her expertise in nutrition science with coaching skills gained through High Performance Master Trainer courses at North Star Academy, she guides clients toward a better life through education, awareness, and personalized wellness strategies. In her workshops and consultations, she draws on nutrition science, positive psychology, and personal experience to help each person discover their unique path to a higher quality of life. Her mission is to support individuals in cultivating a healthy body, calm mind, and greater happiness.

Originally from Tabriz, Iran, Negar was born in 1975 and developed a passion for reading and exploring ways to improve the quality of life from a young age. She studied nutrition science at Tabriz University of Medical Sciences after initially enrolling in chemistry. Following her graduation and internship at the Food Standards Administration, she worked as a quality control officer in various food factories. She completed specialized training in food standards, ISO systems, and quality control of products such as flour and edible oils.

In 2014, she immigrated to Canada and settled in Montreal with her family. After completing further studies at McGill University, she gained experience in several companies before joining a food supply chain company, where she contributed to the global distribution of healthy, safe, and high-quality food.

Negar believes that flourishing and good health are the rights of all people—and that through awareness and conscious choices, anyone can become the best version of themselves.

Ways to contact the author:

[in] negar-dianat
[O] flourishing_with_negar

The Art of Flourishing
Meaning, Growth, and Resilience When Life Isn't Easy

Shervin Esfandyari

The Art of Flourishing
Meaning, Growth, and Resilience When Life Isn't Easy

Shervin Esfandyari
Clinical Psychologist, Coach, and Trainer

Learning to Live Again After Immigration

I am an immigrant woman who, in my home country, had the opportunity to grow and advance—both personally and professionally—by relying on my strengths, the support of my community and family, and the power of conscious choices.

Life in a familiar land gave me the space to create meaning and to claim a clear place for myself. But with the beginning of my immigration journey, it felt as though I had stepped into a completely new and unfamiliar world—a place where I had to relearn the very alphabet of living. Like a toddler, I found myself learning again how to walk, speak, and understand the subtle codes of a new culture. The difference was that I wasn't a blank page; my mind carried a lifetime of experiences, lessons, and stories. This inner cargo felt like a heavy backpack—sometimes slowing me down on the new path, sometimes keeping me steady. I couldn't set it aside, and truthfully, I didn't want to, for it was part of my identity. At times, it filled me with confidence; at other times, it deepened my sense of longing and homesickness.

Years have passed, and I no longer carry that backpack on my shoulders. I have transformed it into a beautiful, deep, and secure chest within me. It is no longer a weight but a treasure holding all that I have been, learned, and lived. This chest is a wellspring of insight and inspiration—a reminder of my roots that helps me bloom even in new soil. Over time, I've learned that when homesickness stirs within me, a short pause, a few slow breaths, and naming three things I am grateful for in this very moment bring me back to the solid ground of now.

What Is My Role?

If I were to describe my lived experiences since immigrating, I must admit that these years have involved navigating a new and dynamic world—a world that, from the onset of the COVID pandemic to today, has continuously opened new and unknown doors. During this time, it feels as though existence sheds its skin every day. These transformations—sometimes breathtaking and sometimes draining—profoundly alter life, encompassing social and political shifts as well as economic, educational, and technological changes.

Living at the heart of such a world has filled me with conflicting emotions: happiness and sadness, hope and doubt, peace and turmoil. This experience has impacted not only my inner world but also my relationships and the overall quality of my life.

In these years, alongside economic crises, political tensions, and the acceleration of technology, the educational system and the workplace have also transformed, particularly with the rise and accessibility of artificial intelligence. Amidst all this, deep questions have formed in my mind:

Where do I stand amidst these changes? What is my role in this emerging world? Should I be a mere spectator or a conscious participant? Should I resist, or should I adapt along with the changes? These questions are not just personal concerns; they are integral to my human journey—a quest to find my unique meaning, direction, and role in a world that is birthing something new every day.

Today, I perceive my role in multiple dimensions. Sometimes, I am an empathetic listener; at other times, a facilitator for change, and occasionally, a source of hope. My role is constantly being redefined, just as the world around me continues to evolve. Whenever doubt arises, I gently open that cherished chest, and the scent of old letters, the warmth of faded photos, and the names of those who once touched my heart flood back. Those memories help me stand firm today. Each time I reach into that chest, my role becomes clearer.

Pain and Awareness: My Path to Self-Actualization

I want to make a sincere confession to the reader of this book: initially, confronting the instability and changes of life after immigration was confusing and vague for me. My unclear understanding of the existing conditions led to mental turmoil and awakened feelings that initially seemed unpleasant but were rooted in something more profound: pain. Yes, real pain.

It was not merely sadness but a sign of something more—a warning from my psyche, from a part of me that had always been ignored. It was pain that compelled me to pause, to reflect, and then to set out in a new direction. In that stillness, I understood that if I silenced its voice, I would remain imprisoned in a cycle of repeated suffering. This was not mere discomfort—it was an awakening, a deeper awareness that every pain carries within it a message. Physical and emotional pains are whispers of a hidden wound, the echo of an unconscious choice, a step taken on the wrong path, or an injury left unattended. I came to see that pain is not something to be denied nor endured passively, but embraced as an invitation to change. My intention isn't to endorse suffering but to acknowledge its presence.

Pain became a guide for me—a light that sought out and revealed the cause and root of my suffering in the darkness of my psyche. This perspective encouraged me to face reality instead of fleeing from it and to build a new path from within. From those days, I ingrained a simple but effective exercise in my mind: whenever a wave of pain arose, I would name it, locate it in my body, and ask myself, "What is this pain trying to remind me of?" The answers weren't always immediate, but this dialogue helped reduce my sense of helplessness.

On my path to healing, I walked alongside others who had also experienced similar pains. My sense of empathy deepened, allowing me to understand not only my own pain but also the pain of others. This shared experience deepened our human connection and taught me the importance of setting clear boundaries with others, allowing space for healing. Healing became a moment-by-moment journey, much like a bone that strengthens as it mends. Now I believe that pain, if we don't get lost in it and allow it to define us, can awaken us. However, if we become one with it, we risk deep and exhausting suffering—a suffering that keeps us trapped in darkness and fatigue.

Awareness of pain and the ability to give it meaning deepen life and pave the way to self-actualization. The conscious experience of pain, especially during challenging times such as immigration and global crises, can transform into an inner force for growth, change, and reconstruction. Realistic acceptance of change and attributing meaning to suffering were integral to my growth journey, but they were not the entirety of it. To truly flourish, I needed to redefine myself—not based on external desires, but on authentic inner ones. I asked myself: "What is within my control in this situation? What is the smallest possible step?" The answers were often simple: an honest conversation, a short walk, or writing a few lines. I had to establish a foundation for self-actualization that began with accepting pain and continued with a commitment to growth.

I devised a plan for myself: five minutes of free writing each morning, a thirty-second pause at noon to check in with my body and acknowledge my feelings, and an evening review of a difficult situation using three short questions: "What happened? How did I feel? What is the smallest next step?"

This straightforward routine made my decisions actionable.

Flourishing in a Changing World: A Lived and Learning Experience

For me, flourishing is not a static concept nor dependent on ideal conditions; it is a dynamic and evolving journey. The meaning of flourishing in my life is about becoming the best possible version of myself—not in comparison to others, but in relation to my past self.

This path relies on finding meaning in experiences, growing amidst challenges, and building resilience in the face of life's turmoil. Flourishing occurs not only in pleasant moments but also in the heart of difficulties. Every pain is an opportunity for deeper understanding, and every ambiguity lays the groundwork for an open mind. For me, being my best is relative; it's not absolute or static, but a continuous and flexible process—a growth that unfolds in the context of change, not in complete stability.

In a world characterized by a dizzying pace of transformations—from social and technological shifts to cultural and climatic changes—humans are compelled to learn new skills, reevaluate their beliefs, and adapt to emerging needs. This adaptation does not imply passivity; rather, it represents a conscious and flexible response to new conditions. I have learned that any change that frightens me becomes more manageable when broken down into small, actionable steps. Whenever I return to my personal values, I have a compass to differentiate between my options.

The pressure of transformation can lead to anxiety and mental exhaustion, but it is precisely at this juncture that inner strength becomes essential. For me, sustaining that strength means nurturing my mental energy: getting enough sleep, setting healthy boundaries in relationships, and intentionally engaging in activities that create meaning. In my experience, growth and adaptability are deeply intertwined. Each time I have faced life's powerful challenges, an opportunity for self-actualization has emerged. With every encounter with change, I have uncovered a new ability within myself. This conscious confrontation with uncertainty has taught me that even in the midst of instability, I can cultivate inner stability.

In such a world, the meaning of life is no longer defined solely by external successes; rather, it is shaped by our responses to adversity, the quality of our relationships, and the depth of our self-awareness. Flourishing means becoming a meaningful, resilient, and evolving human, even in the midst of storms. This perspective transforms every change from a threat into an opportunity for self-recreation. Each time I forget this truth, I rely on a calm breath, small steps, and a return to my values to regain my direction. This simple trio serves as my daily compass, guiding me back to my main path even on the busiest of days.

Purpose and Resilience: A Practical Guide to Conscious Living

I believe that when a person infuses their life with meaning and purpose, they can navigate a clear path even in times of turmoil. In our rapidly changing and unpredictable world, living without purpose is akin to a rudderless boat adrift in a stormy sea. Constant and unclear changes can push individualsout of their comfort zones—a space characterized by control, predictability, and peace. While leaving this comfort zone often brings fear and anxiety, it can also serve as the catalyst for genuine growth.

A person who is aware of their emotions is more balanced in the face of change. They recognize their feelings and do not suppress them; instead, they skillfully regulate their emotions to better understand life situations. For me, "accurately naming the feeling"—whether I'm experiencing sadness, shame, anger, or grief—has been a gateway to clearer decisions.

Emotional self-awareness is the key to strengthening our capacity to withstand life's challenges. It means being able to handle psychological pressures, maintain flexibility, and recover after setbacks or crises. Someone with this inner strength not only rises after each crisis but also grows stronger with every challenge. For me, connecting goals with authentic values and breaking them down into small daily steps has been the most effective way to prevent burnout.

Instead of avoiding challenges, a purposeful person analyzes the situation and asks empowering questions: "What is within my control right now? Which choice aligns more with my values? What is the smallest next step?" In practice, I use "If..., then...": "If anxiety rises, then I will take three deep breaths and contact a trusted person." Additionally, each night, I engage in a three-point gratitude practice to reinforce a positive mindset and close the day. Every week, I do a ten-minute review: What did I learn? What worked? What needs to be adjusted? And what is the small step for the next week? These brief pauses truly keep me on a positive growth journey.

For me, purpose and emotional self-awareness are the two pillars of conscious living. These two qualities have helped me to move my life forward in a meaningful and constructive way, rather than becoming trapped in a cycle of suffering and burnout, even when the world seems to be falling apart. This is precisely where a spark of hope is born from the heart of despair.

From Pain to Power: A Summary from a Psychologist, Coach, and Trainer

As a clinical psychologist, personal development coach, and trainer on flourishing, I believe that the concept of flourishing extends beyond fleeting moments of happiness and external successes. True flourishing encompasses the ability to live with awareness, meaning, flexibility, and resilience in the heart of realities that are sometimes difficult and complex.

In **Positive Psychology**, flourishing is a multidimensional process that involves personal growth, commitment to values, connection with others, finding meaning in life, and constructively facing challenges. Flourishing does not imply the absence of pain; rather, it is about navigating through pain while maintaining hope, meaning, and purpose.

In my professional view, resilience is not a fixed trait but a learned skill that can be cultivated and strengthened. This involves regulating emotions, embracing cognitive flexibility, practicing self-compassion during difficult moments, leaning on support networks, and establishing small but sustainable habits. When goals are clearly defined, measurable, and broken down into manageable steps, the experience of "small successes" fuels larger achievements.

My experiences have shown that the dark and painful aspects of life, when properly understood and processed, can become sources of inner strength. In my practice, I combine emotion-regulation exercises, cognitive restructuring, daily mindfulness, and value-aligned actions to create a reliable foundation for resilience—one that guides individuals toward meaning and choice instead of dwelling in suffering.

Flourishing is about movement, not stagnation; it is about depth, not superficiality. A flourishing individual simultaneously accepts limitations and realities while also envisioning a clear future and consciously taking responsibility for their life with courage. This courage is not carelessness; it involves relying on internal and external evidence: listening to the body, examining thoughts, testing new behaviors on a small scale, and adjusting based on feedback.

I believe that in today's fast-paced and sometimes unstable world, flourishing is not only possible but essential for maintaining mental health, enhancing quality of life, and creating a more humane society. I apply this approach in my workshops and coaching sessions by aligning goals with values, strengthening self-regulation skills, and building small but consistent routines that make change sustainable.

This book invites you on a journey toward conscious and meaningful living in unstable times, transforming pain into power and ambiguity into clarity. If there is one takeaway from these pages, it is this: each of us can create a more livable tomorrow through honest observation, choices aligned with our values, and small steps taken today.

The Art of Flourishing
Meaning, Growth, and Resilience When Life Isn't Easy

About the Author

Shervin Esfandyari is a clinical psychologist, coach, and trainer. Her work focuses on coaching for personal growth and teaching the principles of flourishing, and is certified by the International Coaching Federation.

Shervin holds a master's degree in business administration (MBA) and has spent many years in management roles that prioritize a human-centered and aesthetic approach, aiming to enhance the quality of human presence and enrich the experience of life. She has consistently sought to bridge the gap between managerial thinking and the profound depths of psychology—a combination that connects executive decisions to human insights.

In response to today's fast-paced world, Shervin has determined that her path of influence lies in the coexistence of management and psychology. As a result, she has directed her professional efforts toward coaching and positive psychology, guiding individuals on their journeys toward meaning, balance, and self-actualization.

Shervin's long-standing passion for art, particularly acting and voice acting, serves as a vibrant and independent avenue for her—providing opportunities for narration, role immersion, voice training, and an awareness of the body and rhythm. These experiences have enriched her understanding of emotion, storytelling, movement, and sound, fostering a more authentic connection with her audience.

In her professional practice, Shervin draws upon **Positive Psychology** and **Coaching**, emphasizing the discovery of strengths, meaning, and resilience while translating insights into actionable steps aligned with values. She believes that every individual carries the seeds of flourishing within them, which can blossom into meaning and balance in an environment of awareness, acceptance, and growth.

This book is her second work and a continuation of her first, written in the years following her immigration—an invitation to live consciously in uncertain times and to find meaning amidst ambiguity.

You can contact Shervin by:

✉ shervincoach@gmail.com
◉ shervin.coaching

A Home Across the Waters
Flourishing Through Future-Minded Property Investment

Amirhossein Hajigholami

A Home Across the Waters
Flourishing Through Future-Minded Property Investment

Amirhossein Hajigholami
Strategic Consultant and Trusted Companion in International Investment

The Journey to Flourishing

The journey toward financial flourishing often begins with a bold step into the unknown. For me, this first step was discovering the opportunities hidden in international markets, particularly in North Cyprus. My acquaintance with this island began when a friend invited me there for a business consultation. But what I saw upon arrival was far more than an economic project: warm and hospitable people, an environment of unparalleled tranquility, and opportunities waiting to be discovered in every corner.

Since 2021, I have traveled many times to different regions of North Cyprus. I have immersed myself in the daily lives of people, gained firsthand understanding of laws and regulations, and grappled with the challenges of the market. These experiences have taught me that successful and ethical investment requires deep knowledge, patience, and the companionship of an experienced advisor.

What you will read in this chapter is a combination of real

experiences and key insights that can make your investment path more transparent, safer, and more profitable.

Real Stories, Real Flourishing: Principles of Diverse Investments

Sometimes, a single real experience is enough to transform your future from doubt to certainty and from a dream to reality.

Story 1: The Foundation of Prudence and Informed Risk

A young couple, hoping to build a secure future and explore new horizons, was captivated by an investment opportunity promoted with deceptive slogans like "High returns with minimal risk!" Without conducting in-depth research or consulting an expert, they invested a substantial portion of their savings based solely on these promises.

At first, everything seemed perfect: projections of rapid growth, promises of guaranteed profits, and easy entry conditions. But behind the scenes, the main asset lacked valid legal documentation, and the project was struggling with unresolved issues. When they attempted to withdraw their capital, they faced the harsh reality of losing a significant portion of their money.

This experience is a reminder of a simple truth: flourishing does not mean avoiding risk entirely, but instead accepting *informed risk*—where perseverance, thorough research, and credible advice act as your protective shield. Genuine flourishing is built on a foundation of verified information and choices that ensure your long-term security and peace of mind.

Story 2: Beyond Return on Investment: Creating a Balanced Life and Purposeful Wealth

A seasoned business professional with years of experience was feeling suffocated by the relentless pressure of urban life and his high-level job responsibilities. He was looking for more than just financial growth; he needed a place for rest and recovery.

After careful evaluation and consultation with specialists, he decided to invest in a quiet, coastal property in a growing area, such as Long Beach, North Cyprus. His choice was intelligent: the property had high potential for rental income and also served as a personal sanctuary to escape the daily hustle. Today, he enjoys a rare combination: financial stability and inner peace. His investment works for him nonstop, while he recharges in his seaside retreat.

This is the meaning of *purposeful wealth*: making financial decisions that not only yield economic returns but also align with personal values, creating a life where tranquility, stress reduction, and more opportunities to pursue one's passions hold a special place.

Story 3: The Importance of Foresight, Trustworthiness, and Legal Security

A recently retired woman was seeking an opportunity to convert her life savings into a stable investment. One day, a tempting offer caught her ear: "Impressive returns, along with a delightful lifestyle by the sea." The promoter said with a reassuring smile, "Everything is in order, just sign this preliminary agreement."

Excitement and trust replaced due diligence. Without consulting an independent lawyer or verifying official registration and relying only on a captivating story and a handwritten note, she made a major financial commitment. She did not know that in North Cyprus, official registration at the Tapu (Land Registry) Office is a vital step that guarantees ownership security. Months passed. There was no news of the promised progress, nor the peace she sought. Finally, the reality became clear: the property lacked the necessary legal approvals, and her investment was left entirely unprotected.

This woman's experience reminds us that true flourishing is not built on immediate pleasures alone; it requires foresight, the use of reliable resources, and reliance on professional advice. In international investments, especially in real estate, nothing replaces clear and official legal registration. Promises and verbal agreements, without a legal framework and valid registration, are much like paper boats: beautiful at first glance, but powerless against the first wave.

Story 4: Strategic Investment for Personal Freedom and Stability

A middle-aged couple, having retired after years of work, dreamed of a peaceful life in a country with a pleasant climate and reasonable costs. They wanted to find a place that offered not only tranquility but also legal and financial security.

With patience and care, they reviewed various options for obtaining long-term residency through investment. Ultimately, after consulting with experts, they made a calculated decision: to purchase a fully legal property with all necessary documentation in a stable and popular region, such as Famagusta in North Cyprus.

The result of this foresight was a deep sense of peace. The residency process was completed quickly and without complications, allowing them to begin a new chapter of their lives, free from worries about their residency status and financial future.

As stated in Maslow's hierarchy of needs, safety and security are essential foundations for moving toward higher levels of self-actualization. When this base is solid, it frees up the energy and mind to engage more joyfully with relationships, new experiences, and personal interests.

Story 5: Investing for Generational Flourishing: A Legacy of Opportunity

Forward-thinking parents had a clear vision for their family:

to provide a secure foundation for their child's financial independence and access to international opportunities.

After carefully considering various global investment options, they made a wise choice: purchasing a fully legal property with stable income potential near a reputable university in North Cyprus. This was not just a financial investment but part of a strategic plan to support their child's educational and life journey.

Years later, this decision bore fruit. The rental income from the property covered a major portion of their child's tuition and living expenses. Furthermore, the home became a safe and stable base for him, a place that fostered a sense of stability and belonging during his studies.

This story demonstrates that conscious investment can create a lasting legacy that extends beyond one generation. For parents who prioritize their children's future, there is no sweeter reward than seeing them grow and succeed—a success rooted in the thoughtful planning and decisions of today.

Story 6: Beyond the Surface: The Search for True Value

A young, experienced, and successful entrepreneur was always drawn to projects presented with glamour, stunning images, and promises of luxury. On one of his trips to an emerging market, he saw a project that was captivating in every way—from its glossy brochures and exclusive amenities to its flexible payment terms. But amidst these attractions, the most important question remained unanswered: was there real, legal value behind this charming facade?

When he began to investigate with a more critical eye, the truth was revealed: the project lacked essential permits and was entangled in complex legal disputes. He was able to get his initial financial commitment back, but it took months and created immense psychological pressure.

This experience reminded him, and us, that appearances can be deceiving, but security and lasting value lie in the substance and authenticity of an investment. Just as positive psychology highlights the difference between fleeting pleasure and deep-seated contentment, in investing, we must look past momentary temptations and rely on real, legal foundations.

Story 7: The Balance Between Dream and Reality

A couple, passionate about nature and tranquility, enthusiastically bought a property in a remote, scenic area. In their minds, they pictured a peaceful, self-sufficient life filled with beauty. However, after the move, reality revealed a different face: an unstable internet connection, lengthy commutes to essential services such as schools and medical centers, and limited access to basic amenities. Their dream gradually gave way to disappointment and a sense of isolation. Eventually, they were forced to sell the property and, due to its unfavorable location, accept a significant financial loss.

Natural beauty and peace are valuable, but this experience is a reminder of a crucial truth for a successful life and flourishing decisions: essential infrastructure, easy access to services, and daily comfort must also be present. Major investments that impact lifestyle will only be sustainable and satisfying when both dreams and practical realities are considered side by side.

Story 8: The Power of Timely and Informed Decision-Making

A young professional with a modest budget was lost in a sea of information and sometimes contradictory advice. During a consultation with his trusted expert, he was introduced to an opportunity in a new and growing market, like the Long Beach area in North Cyprus. This region had high growth potential due to ongoing infrastructure projects and government support. Relying on the expert's analysis and his own personal research, he decided to act without delay.

Only a short time later, the value of his investment saw significant growth, proving that decisive action based on knowledge can bring remarkable results.

This story is a key reminder: uncertainty should not become an excuse for inaction. Success often lies in the ability to combine careful analysis with the boldness to seize the right moments—not by acting recklessly, but by making smart, timely decisions.

Story 9: Investment Aligned with Life's Reality

A retired couple was initially drawn to luxurious, glamorous projects advertised with impressive images and a long list of amenities. But with a little reflection and smart consultation, they realized these options were compatible with neither their simple, unpretentious lifestyle nor their carefully managed budget.

Ultimately, they decided to focus on a practical and fully legal option: a property that provided daily comfort, easy access to essential services, and financial security. Today, they live with peace of mind, confident that their choice aligns perfectly with their needs and the realities of their life, not with an advertised dream.

This experience demonstrates that external pressures and enticing promises often present a distorted picture of an "ideal life" that may be far from reality. True flourishing takes shape when our investments align completely with our values, preferences, and financial circumstances. This alignment brings peace, lasting satisfaction, and a sense of self-acceptance.

Story 10: From Adversity to Purpose: A Catalyst for Change

A close friend of mine started down an investment path that, unfortunately, led to a costly mistake. He trusted an unofficial intermediary and was deceived by attractive but misleading advertising. The investment lacked legal documentation and was based on an unstable project. I witnessed his sleepless nights, his anxiety over losing his capital, and his deep sense of helplessness. But instead of just watching, this experience became a powerful motivation for me to act.

This bitter challenge illuminated a pressing need: the existence of a trustworthy and knowledgeable guide for people navigating the complexities of international investment. This experience strengthened my personal commitment to use my knowledge and background in strategic consulting to support and guide others, turning my friend's adversity into a catalyst for building a safer and brighter future for many.

A commitment to service and building a foundation of trust aligns with the principles of positive psychology, including concepts such as meaning and purpose. It shows how, from personal challenges, a powerful force for collective good and deeper flourishing can be created.

Your Investment Roadmap: Steps to Flourishing

Investing in a new opportunity or a new place is more than a financial decision; it is a journey toward a different and meaningful future. Here is a step-by-step guide to help you move forward on this path with confidence and awareness.

1. **Clearly Define Your Goals and Choose the Right Location:** First, determine exactly what your objective is: income, capital growth, residency, or a lifestyle change. Then, select markets and regions that align with these goals. For instance, certain areas in North Cyprus might be best for your specific objectives, just as different asset classes in global

markets pursue other goals.

2. **Conduct Thorough and Comprehensive Due Diligence:** Before any financial commitment, carefully verify the legal status, ownership, and regulatory compliance of the investment. This critical stage may include reviewing title deeds, necessary permits, financial statements, and other relevant documents.

3. **Seek Expert and Independent Consultation:** Never proceed without the guidance of a professional and impartial advisor who specializes in the investment field, local laws, and the market. This advisor will accompany you through the complexities of the path.

4. **Structure Secure and Realistic Payments:** Payment terms should be transparent, legal, and proportionate to your financial capacity. If necessary, explore options for phased payments and secure transactions.

5. **Formalize and Protect Your Investment:** Complete all legal registrations and documentation related to your ownership and rights. For property investments, this includes official registration in the relevant departments. In other types of investments, the registration of contracts and shares is mandatory.

A Reflection on Designing a Flourishing Life

Investment, whether in property or any other significant

asset, is not just about money; it is about *life design*. It is an opportunity to pause, reflect, and ask yourself: "What kind of future do I truly want to build?"

When we align our investments with our deepest values—freedom, family, learning, travel, or any other important principle—we are, in fact, opening the path to flourishing. We transform from passive earners into active architects of our own lives.

Through years of accompanying various clients, I have learned that flourishing is a personal and unique journey that begins with a single question: "What future do you want to arrive at?"

Take time today to think carefully—not only about your money, but also about your precious time, energy, and dreams. Do your investments and your choices align with the life you desire? If the answer is no, perhaps it is time to discover new paths.

Whether that path involves strategic investment in real estate or investing in education and personal development, every decision you make for your future is an essential step toward a more prosperous and more flourishing existence.

A Home Across the Waters

Flourishing Through Future-Minded Property Investment

About the Author

Amirhossein Hajigholami is a

strategic consultant and a trusted companion in international investment. With over 26 years of extensive experience, he has skillfully guided countless individuals and organizations through the complex landscapes of international trade, sophisticated business development, and strategic investment. A distinguished graduate in Management from Tarbiat Modares University, Amirhossein combines a great wealth of academic knowledge with deep practical insights gained from his real-world application.

His professional philosophy is built on one fundamental, unwavering principle: empowering informed decision-making. He firmly believes in meticulously analyzing each client's unique circumstances and always looking toward their brightest future, rather than promoting hasty or ill-considered choices that could lead to regret. Amirhossein is renowned for his solid commitment to analytical rigor, immense courage, and innovative creativity in taking control during the most challenging crises. For him, a problem is never the end of the road; it is inherently the beginning of a solution. His personal journey into international markets, particularly his vivid and formative experiences in North Cyprus, has enriched his pragmatic approach, allowing him to offer guidance rooted in his firsthand knowledge of diverse regulations, dynamic market forces, and cultural nuances.

Amirhossein's personal mission was profoundly reinforced by witnessing a close friend's costly investment mistake. That challenging experience became the decisive catalyst for Amirhossein to establish **G99 Group – A Golden Choice for Informed Investment**. The mission of G99 Group extends far beyond mere transactions; it was fundamentally formed to offer support to individuals seeking to make informed, secure, and peaceful investment decisions. While its initial focus has been on expertly navigating the complexities of emerging markets, such as North Cyprus, its vision is ambitiously set to expand its trusted guidance across other growing international territories, including the United Arab Emirates and beyond.

G99 Group is committed to being by your side through every stage of this vital journey, from the very first exploratory step to any moment you might need ongoing support. G99 Group ensures that feelings of isolation, uncertainty, or doubt do not cloud your path or hinder your progress. You are not just investing in assets; you are building a secure future, cultivating lasting well-being, and achieving true flourishing.

The Right Decision Needs the Right Guide.

Connect with G99 Group:

+90539-109-8420 | +90539-110-8420
www.G99.biz
G99.biz
G99.ngo@gmail.com

The Power of Small, Sustainable, and Consistent Changes

An Inner Wave—Gentle Yet Powerful—that Begins with the Tiniest Drop and Flows Toward Sustainable Flourishing

Maryam Kai Kabir

The Power of Small, Sustainable, and Consistent Changes

An Inner Wave—Gentle Yet Powerful—that Begins with the Tiniest Drop and Flows Toward Sustainable Flourishing

Maryam Kai Kabir

Author, Regeneration Coach, Psychologist, and Researcher

Let's begin this chapter with a couple of **questions** worth sitting with:

- If nothing in your **life changes** from this moment on, what might you lose five years from now?
- And if you **start** just one small change - no matter how subtle - today, where might you be standing in five years' time?

The Quiet Force Within

In today's world—crowded with crises, uncertainty, and an undercurrent of restlessness—everything seems to shout: "Faster! More! Better!"

All too often, we absorb that shout until it echoes inside us. We keep running, not always toward our dreams, but sometimes simply to escape the fear of falling behind or losing control.

But what if, just for a moment, we stopped to ask: Is all this speed truly carrying us where we want to go? Or is the deeper power tucked away in something simpler, quieter, and perhaps even unseen?

My own journey of transformation began the day I realized that many of my immediate reactions were fueled by anxiety. When I felt under threat, I would reach for the first solution that came to mind, rarely the most conscious or effective one. And when that failed, the self-blame would pour in:

"You've failed again."

"See? You never really change."

"You're simply not cut out for this."

What I've witnessed again and again—in coaching sessions, in scientific findings, and in everyday life—is this: when change begins as a drop, it endures. And when true strength is born from mindful consistency—not from an emotional impulse—it sends its roots far deeper.[1]

This chapter is about that kind of strength. The kind that may seem "small" at first glance, but when paired with awareness, steady repetition, kindness, and time, can quietly rebuild a life from the ground up. There's nothing magical here. We're talking about moments and actions that feel aligned with who we really are.

Together, we'll explore scientific research and the kinds of small habits that work silently yet powerfully, carrying us from burnout to blossoming. This isn't just theory; it's lived

---

1. Doidge, N. (2007). *The Brain That Changes Itself.* Viking Press.

and tested experience.

It's also an invitation:

A return to the roots.

A return to your inner rhythm.

A return to those tiny drops you may have forgotten, but which are still here, waiting for their moment to flow again.

Now, it's your turn:

- √ Have you ever paused to notice which quiet little habit has been shaping your life?

The Logic Behind Small Changes

In a world obsessed with quick fixes and instant success, we often overlook the quiet force of gradual impact.

Yet nature tells a different story:

- Drops of water, with patience and repetition, can carve through stone not by force, not by speed, but through steady persistence.
- A ship that shifts its course by even one degree, if it keeps moving, can arrive at a completely different continent months later.

This is the philosophy behind small, conscious changes. They are the ones that guide us back home to our truest selves.

The Three-Step Model of Small Change

Over the course of my coaching journey, after witnessing hundreds of real-life transformations, a quiet pattern began to emerge, one that now flows through the **Florynthia** Wave Model.[1] It was a path not built from grand, sweeping changes, but from three gentle waves:

1. Stillness: Creating space to pause, listen inward, and observe recurring patterns.
2. Shifting: Making a small, intentional move grounded in awareness.
3. Sustaining: Repeating a micro-change until it sparks inner shifts—like a sense of capability or fulfillment—that gradually become part of one's identity.

Though subtle in appearance, these three stages hold profound transformative power.

They are rooted in resilience, inner restoration, and sustainable flourishing, and over time they weave themselves naturally into the rhythm of our being.

Resilience within the Waves of Change

Resilience is often described as "rising after the fall," but in the world of small changes, it comes with a shift in perspective.

---

1. The Florynthia Wave Model, rooted in the Kai Kabir philosophy, is a six-phase model for inner transformation and sustainable flourishing. This chapter flows through three of its core waves: Stillness, Shifting, and Sustaining.

On this path, we step back, get tired, or forget—again and again. Yet because these changes are light and manageable, the way back is always open.

"Resilience is not a trait only some people possess. It involves behaviors, thoughts, and actions that can be learned and developed by anyone."[1]

"Real change doesn't scream or sprint. It falls softly, drop by drop..., until one day, you wake up and realize your soil is no longer dry." —Kai Kabir

Now, it's your turn:

- √ Think of a recent challenge you've faced.
- √ Write down three recurring behaviors that haven't worked.
- √ Now define one very small step that would be different (e.g., if you always stay silent, say one sentence. If you usually react, pause just once).
- √ Practice that small change for three days and reflect on what happens.

What Science Says

Recent research in neuroscience and behavioral psychology shows that small, gradual changes are often more lasting, likely because of their gentle yet sustainable impact on the brain's adaptive systems.[2]

---

1. Bonanno, G. A. (2004). Loss, trauma, and human resilience. *American Psychologist, 59*(1), 20–28.
2. Doidge, N. (2007). *The brain that changes itself: Stories of*

When you make a change that is small, doable, and paired with an intrinsic reward, the limbic system—the brain's center for emotion, motivation, and survival—records it as safe and repeatable.

The brain is constantly reshaping itself through a process called neuroplasticity. Every thought, decision, and action leaves a trace of neural activity.[1]

When that path is repeated often, it forms a network that makes the new behavior easier and more automatic. For example, someone who sits quietly for just two minutes a day may stop needing reminders after a few weeks. The brain begins to treat this habit as part of its survival system—because it brings clarity and calm.[2]

Dopamine Theory and Inner Pleasure

"Dopamine neurons respond to rewards and reward-predicting stimuli with bursts of activity, and to the absence of expected rewards with a drop in activity."[3]

In simple terms, when a behavior leads to a rewarding feeling, dopamine acts as a natural motivator, encouraging us to repeat that behavior. This means that even small actions, if they

personal triumph from the frontiers of brain science. Viking Press.
1. Schwartz, J. M; Begley, S. (2002). *The mind and the brain: Neuroplasticity and the power of mental force.* Harper Perennial.
2. Rock, D. (2009). *Your brain at work: Strategies for overcoming distraction, regaining focus, and working smarter all day long.* Harper Business.
3. Schultz, W. (2015). Neuronal reward and decision signals: From theories to data. *Physiological Reviews, 95*(3), 853–951.

trigger genuine satisfaction, can set off a positive feedback loop that makes the habit easier to sustain.

Hope Theory

Hope is one of the most powerful forces for change. Psychologist Charles Snyder[1] proposed a model of hope built on three key elements:

- Goal – Something we care deeply about
- Pathways – The possible routes to get there
- Agency – The belief that we can move along that path

Small changes naturally activate all three. When the goal is clear yet manageable, the path becomes visible and repeatable, and our belief in our ability to grow is strengthened.

Now, it's your turn:

- √ Choose one behavior you've been wanting to change for a while.
- √ Reduce it to a single small, concrete step (For example: instead of "exercise every day," decide on "one stretch per day.")
- √ After doing it, write down how you feel. Did you notice any satisfaction or a sense of control?
- √ Track that feeling each day and watch how your inner dopamine begins to coach you forward.

---

1. Snyder, C. R. (2002). Hope theory. Rainbows in the mind. *Psychological Inquiry, 13*(4), 249–275.

Real-Life Stories of Small Changes

– Just One Simple Question

Sara, 36, had a long history of unfinished decisions. In her first coaching session, after a brief silence and a deep sigh, she said: "I'm always waiting for something big to happen so I can change... but I always miss the moment."

So I asked her one question: "If you had just ten minutes a day that belonged only to you, what would you do with it?"

From that day, she began writing her thoughts for ten minutes each day.

Three weeks later, she said: "For the first time, I feel I understand myself."

Later, she added: "Those ten minutes became the gateway to my lost self-confidence."

– The Trace of Doubt

Amir, a startup executive, looked successful on the outside but was worn down by decision fatigue.

"I'm successful at work," he said, "but I feel no joy, just ticking boxes."

Our sessions felt like carefully calculated chess moves, but without any soul. I suggested he walk in nature for five minutes a day, with no goal attached.

He laughed. "Waste my time?" But he tried it anyway.

By the fifth session, his face was lighter. "I walk every day now. Work pressures are still there, but those walks let my mind breathe, and I feel better."

- **The Flowers That Saved Him**

Mr. Nouri, a retired man, lived alone in silence after his wife's passing.

In our first session, he said: "I don't think anything will change."

I asked: "If you could do something that feels good, what would it be?"

He paused, then said: "I've always loved gardening, but now it feels meaningless." I suggested he spend a few minutes each day simply looking at his flowers.

Weeks later, he told me softly: "I thought I was taking care of the flowers, but they were taking care of me." Now, he spends half an hour in the garden daily, planting with his granddaughter and greeting life from his window.

- **The Moment Everything Should Have Ended but Began**

At 28, my body became motionless. Walking—a simple act—felt like climbing a distant mountain. Doctors told me gently: "You may never walk the same again."

When my limbs wouldn't move, my mind filled with dark questions:

"Why me?"

"What now?"

"Is this the end?"

One early morning, before sunrise, a thought cut through the pain: "If one small movement could pull you out of this darkness... would you do it?"

My answer was "Yes." That day, I began moving only the toe of my right foot. This time it wasn't pain; it was hope. Each small movement became a fresh drop bringing me closer to the ground of my being. It felt as if the universe replied, and a doctor full of light entered my life. Step by step, I rose again not only on my feet but onto a new ground I called Self-Regeneration. Writing this chapter today doesn't mean I've only become "strong"; it means I've learned that even the smallest movement can spark hope and begin regeneration.

"When nothing else moves, if even a single cell stirs, that is the beginning of life again." —Kai Kabir

Now, it's your turn:

- √ Which story felt closest to you—Sara, Amir, Mr. Nouri, or mine?
- √ What part of your life is quietly asking for a small shift?
- √ Today, give it just five minutes.
  - Sit with that part of you.
  - Listen to its silence.
  - It may whisper where to begin.
  - Maybe it's a toe.

- Maybe a step.
- Maybe a call.
- Maybe a sentence—to yourself.

"At first, small changes may only touch the soil. But if continued, one day, they take root deep in the soul." —Kai Kabir

A Glance at History, and Our World Today

Sometimes, a look back at history can light the path ahead. Again and again, small changes have reshaped the destiny of nations and movements:

- In 1930, Mahatma Gandhi walked 380 kilometers to protest Britain's salt tax. The act—simply gathering salt from the sea—seemed small, yet it became the foundation of India's independence.[1]
- In 1963, Martin Luther King Jr. delivered his iconic "I Have a Dream" speech during a peaceful march in Washington. Through nonviolence, dialogue, and unwavering faith, his steady voice became a wave of awareness that led to landmark civil rights legislation in the United States.[2]
- Socrates, the fifth-century BCE philosopher, never wrote a book. Yet through simple, persistent questioning in the streets of Athens, he awakened minds and laid the foundation for modern critical thinking one small

---

1. Gandhi, M. K. (1993). *The essential Gandhi*. Vintage Books.
2. King, M. L., Jr. (1963). I have a dream [Speech transcript]. American Rhetoric.

question at a time.[1]

- Florence Nightingale, during the Crimean War, tended to wounded soldiers by night, guided only by her lamp. Through consistent acts—from cleaning beds to documenting hygiene data—she redefined care and became the mother of modern nursing, not through revolution, but through compassion, structure, and sustained change.[2]

In all these cases, what began small grew to become both lasting and vast.

Inspiration from the Modern World

Today's world offers similar stories of transformation through small shifts:

- James Clear, author of Atomic Habits, rebuilt his life after a traumatic injury. Instead of surrendering to despair, he committed to improving by just 1% each day. Those small, consistent habits became a global blueprint for sustainable transformation.

- Mel Robbins developed the 5-Second Rule—counting down 5, 4, 3, 2, 1—to disrupt hesitation and spark immediate action. This simple tool has helped millions break free from self-sabotaging patterns.[3]

- Brené Brown, research professor at the University of

---

1. Plato. (1997). *Apology*.
2. Nightingale, F. (1859). *Notes on nursing: What it is and what it is not*.
3. Robbins, M. (2017). *The 5 Second Rule*. Savio Republic.

Houston, launched a worldwide conversation about vulnerability, courage, and emotional honesty, beginning with one heartfelt talk that encouraged people to show up as they are.[1]

"History was made by those who took just one step in their moment of awakening." —Kai Kabir

Now, it's your turn:

- √ Choose one of the people mentioned above and explore the first small step they took.
- √ Then ask yourself: What is my very first small step?
- √ Take that step today; the future begins with it.

A Gentle Invitation to Change, Drop by Drop

Pause for a moment.

If you truly believed that small changes could not only save you but awaken the world around you, would you still be chasing sudden transformations?

Throughout this chapter, we've seen that great change rarely begins with dramatic events. Sometimes, it starts with a pause, a question, or a soft breeze that stirs the leaves.

Small changes give our inner world—our beliefs, our patterns, even our neural pathways—the space to align with a new direction. Within every small shift lies the seed of resilience: not just the strength to endure, but the grace to continue…

---

1. Brown, B. (2012). *Daring Greatly*. Gotham Books.

with heart.[1]

We've explored neuroscience, hope theory, dopamine, real-life stories, and the three-step model of micro-change.

And we've learned this:

You don't need a perfect plan. You don't need permission.

You just need one intentional step, taken with presence.

One question.

One choice.

One breath.

Keep going. Stay flexible. Flow with the waves of missteps, detours, and pauses.

This is how we walk toward sustainable flourishing.

The Florynthian Message:

The world may be uncertain, but you can be its steady point with a single smile, a simple act of care, or one small decision made with intention.

---

1. Duckworth, A. (2016). *Grit: The power of passion and perseverance*. Scribner.

The Power of Small, Sustainable, and Consistent Changes

An Inner Wave - Gentle Yet Powerful - that Begins With the Tiniest Drop and Flows Toward Sustainable Flourishing

About the Author

Maryam Kai Kabir, professionally known as Kai Kabir, is an author, coach, educator, and psychology researcher who has spent over three decades inspiring individuals to transform their lives through personal flourishing and the power of small changes. She is the creator of the Florynthia Model of Micro-Change, a gentle yet profound framework for sustainable growth.

Maryam has studied in the fields of sociology, branding, entrepreneurship, psychology, and business management. She has built a living bridge between modern science, inner wisdom, and lived experience—an integration that defines her work.

Her journey took a pivotal turn in her early twenties during a serious illness. That chapter became the beginning of a quiet revolution in her life, shaped by simple sentences and small, intentional steps. It later gave birth to her coaching method and her unique philosophy on sustainable change.

A formative part of her early career unfolded in the watchmaking industry, where she trained young women and helped build specialized teams. This entrepreneurial experience deepened her understanding of motion, precision, time, and the significance of tiny parts—all of which later influenced her teachings and writings.

Kai Kabir believes that every person can move closer to their core purpose through mindful, consistent repetition.

Her business, coaching programs, and books blend feminine flexibility and creative flow with masculine clarity, strategy, and purposeful direction.

After immigrating to Canada, she continued her work as a Flourishing and Regeneration Coach, supporting individuals and organizations seeking a fresh, authentic beginning.

Her writing and programs invite readers into reflection, action, and self-renewal, combining personal stories, psychological insight, and coaching-based practices to help people build new habits and reach meaningful goals.

"You don't need to change everything. Just take one step each day and let the miracle unfold." —Kai Kabir

Dedicated to my son, whose presence sparked awakening in me, and to all those who - even in the heart of an uncertain world - shed light on my path of flourishing and regeneration.

You can find her books and programs at:

🌐 www.kaikabir.com or on Amazon.

Follow and connect on:

 kaikabircoach
 kaikabircoach
 kaikabircoach
 kaikabircoach

From Surviving to Thriving
A Coaching Guide to Flourishing at Work and Beyond

Mohsen Khaki

From Surviving to Thriving
A Coaching Guide to Flourishing at Work and Beyond

Mohsen Khaki
ICF-Certified Professional Coach and Branding Expert

Resilience or Flourishing? Which path is your organization on?

In organizations, "resilience" means enduring challenges without major performance disruptions. While it helps maintain productivity, resilience merely restores the status quo rather than driving growth.

Flourishing goes beyond resilience. Those who flourish not only adapt to challenges but also grow, learn, and excel. Dr. Martin Seligman defines flourishing through five elements:[1]

- **Positive Emotions:** Motivation and enthusiasm at work
- **Engagement:** Deep connection to tasks
- **Relationships:** Strong workplace interactions
- **Meaning:** Understanding work's value
- **Accomplishment:** Personal growth and progress

The reality is that resilience is only part of the success equation. Organizations that focus solely on resilience often

---
1. Seligman, M.E. (2011). *Flourish: A Visionary New Understanding of Happiness and Well-being.* Simon & Schuster Publishing.

face the following problems:

1. Burnout

In 2017, Uber experienced a wave of sudden resignations due to its highly competitive work culture. Employees complained about relentless pressure and exhausting work hours. The excessive focus on "resilience," without considering the need for personal growth and development, led many talented employees to leave the company. As a result, Uber had to rethink its management model and launch new professional development programs for its employees.[1]

Another example is Zappos, a well-known online shoe retailer that initially had an excellent organizational culture encouraging collaboration and growth among its employees. However, as the company expanded rapidly and demand increased, Zappos placed significant pressure on its employees. This excessive pressure on work-life balance, coupled with a lack of opportunities for training and growth, resulted in burnout among employees.

Therefore, some of Zappos' key employees felt demotivated due to the lack of attention to their personal and professional growth. Reports indicated an increase in employee turnover and decreased job satisfaction in recent years. Zappos also discovered through internal assessments that when employees are under pressure and lack opportunities for growth,

---

1. Bhuiyan, J. (2017). *This is how Uber plans to change its own company culture.* Vox.

productivity declines.[1]

2. Decreased Productivity and Motivation

In the 2000s, Microsoft experienced a decline in creativity and motivation due to its intense competitive culture, where employees had to fight for survival. Internal politics consumed employees, leading them to abandon risk-taking for fear of failure. As a result, Microsoft lagged behind innovations from Apple and Google.[2]

How did Microsoft shift from resilience to flourishing? When Satya Nadella became CEO, he transformed the company's culture by focusing on employee learning and development. He introduced organizational coaching programs and new training courses,[3] which helped Microsoft regain its position as one of the world's most innovative companies.[4]

Nokia, once a leader in the mobile industry, also faced a decline in the 2000s. The main reason was an organizational culture that suppressed creativity and offered no opportunities for learning and innovation. The absence of an open environment for learning and coaching led to stagnant thinking among

---

1. Flony, R. (2016). Zappos CEO Tony Hsieh explains why 18% of employees quit during the company's radical management experiment. *Business Insider*.
2. Eichenwald, K. (2012). *Microsoft's lost decade. Vanity Fair*.
3. Fiegerman, S. (2016). *Microsoft stock hits a new all-time high. Here's why*. CNN Tech.
4. Hobson, N. (2024). Satya Nadella's Microsoft Just Became the Most Valued Company in the World. And It's Thanks to Psychology, Not Tech. Growth mindset and empathy are the reason why Microsoft is back on top. *Inc.com*

employees and hindered creative growth.[1]

Therefore, Apple and Samsung surged ahead by fostering environments that encouraged learning and innovation, while Nokia's market share sharply declined. Later, Nokia's CEO famously remarked, "We did not do anything wrong, but we lost."[2]

3. Increased Employee Turnover

In 2021, Goldman Sachs, the investment bank, faced a crisis due to a high turnover rate among young employees. The primary reason was that employees felt they were burning out without opportunities for growth.[3]

How was this problem solved? Instead of solely focusing on salary increases, Goldman Sachs developed coaching and mentoring programs. This shift helped employees feel they had a clear path for advancement, resulting in a significant decrease in turnover rates.[4]

Another example can be seen in the early 2010s when, despite having top talent, Yahoo failed to provide an environment conducive to growth. A rigid organizational culture, lack of learning opportunities, and absence of coaching and personal

---

1. Doz, Y. L. (2017). The strategic decisions that caused Nokia's failure. *Knowledge@INSEAD*.
2. Butterfield, S. (2016). We didn't do anything wrong, but somehow, we lost... *CUInsight*.
3. Damyanova, V. (2022). Flexibility beats pay as investment banks embrace hybrid work to secure talent. *S&P Global*.
4. Goldman Sachs. (n.d.). *Maximizing the potential of our people*. GoldmanSachs.com.

development programs led many of Yahoo's technical elites to leave the company for competitors like Google and Facebook.[1]

So, over the years, Yahoo transitioned from a tech giant to a company struggling to remain competitive. Ultimately, the company was acquired by Verizon in 2017 and lost many of its top talents.

4. Limited Innovation – Netflix's Experience in Building a Growth Culture

In its early years, Netflix focused solely on "surviving" and feared competing with giants like Blockbuster. However, when the company began investing in employee development and coaching programs, it sparked a transformation in its organizational culture.

As a result, employees felt their ideas were heard, and they had opportunities to grow. This cultural shift led to major innovations, such as the personalized movie recommendation algorithm, and helped Netflix become one of the most successful companies in the world.[2]

A second instance is BlackBerry, once a pioneer in the smartphone market, which remained stagnant in its traditional approach as Apple and Google invested in empowering their employees, creating learning spaces, and supporting new

---

1. Yahoo's brain drain shows a loss of faith in the company. (2016). *The Irish Times*.
2. Aletta. (2024). *Theory meets practice at Netflix: A case study on modern organisational development*. Aletta Focus Marketing.

ideas. BlackBerry employees felt they had no room for growth or innovation, and their new ideas went unheard.[1]

Therefore, Apple and Samsung quickly overtook BlackBerry by attracting top talent and cultivating a culture that encouraged innovation. BlackBerry's market share dropped from 20% in 2009 to less than 1% in 2017.[2]

The Path to Employee Flourishing in Top Organizations

Based on a study by the Gallup Institute, organizations that prioritize personal development and coaching programs have seen a significant increase in employee engagement, an improvement in performance, and a meaningful reduction in turnover.[3]

Gallup surveys have shown that when organizations hold regular and purposeful conversations with employees—especially in the form of coaching—employees are up to 45% less likely to leave their jobs and 65% less likely to look for a new one.[4]

On the other hand, a successful example of implementing a personal development strategy is **Johnson & Johnson**.

---

1. Sekar, N. (2024). *BlackBerry's siloed culture: Case study.* Medium.
2. Rossignol, J. (2017). *BlackBerry hits '0%' market share nearly ten years after iPhone launched.* MacRumors.
3. Harter, J. (2018, July 29). *Employee engagement vs. employee satisfaction and organizational culture.* Gallup.
4. Yi, R. (2024). *Employee retention depends on getting recognition right.* Gallup.

Through its **Energy for Performance (E4P)** program, the company achieved the following outcomes:

- Individuals who completed the program were **25% more likely to receive a promotion** within the following year.
- It was projected that the company would **save nearly $200 million** through reduced turnover by the year 2020.[1]

How Coaching Transforms Employees from Resilience to Flourishing

The article *"The Leader as Coach"* explains that when managers embrace the role of a coach and lead with a supportive approach, they can significantly boost their team's energy, innovation, and commitment.[2]

A study published by BetterUp also shows that employees who feel a strong sense of belonging at work experience, on average, 56% higher job performance, 50% lower risk of turnover, and 75% less absenteeism. As a result, a company with 10,000 employees can save up to $52 million in productivity, and employees are 167% more likely to recommend their employer.[3]

One experience that illustrates these findings occurred while

---

1. Bartz, A. (2018). *This healthcare company determined to have the healthiest employees in the world. J&J.*
2. Ibarra, H., & Scoular, A. (2019). *The leader as coach: How to unleash innovation, energy, and commitment.* Harvard Business Review. https://hbr.org
3. BetterUp. (2019). *Industry-leading research shows companies that fail at belonging lose tens of millions in revenue.* BetterUp.

coaching a project manager at a large company. He faced daily challenges that consumed his thoughts: How could he accelerate progress? How could he prevent his team from getting stuck in details? Lacking answers, he even doubted his ability to succeed as a manager. I vividly recall a session where he needed to make critical team decisions but felt paralyzed by uncertainty. I asked, "Imagine you're making a career-defining decision but feel incapable of doing so." He paused, looked into the distance, and admitted, "I doubt myself. I might fail." However, after months of coaching focused on recognizing his strengths and refining his decision-making skills, he gained confidence. He not only led complex projects successfully but also emerged as a leader guiding his team toward growth and success.

Another client, a marketing manager in a high-pressure, competitive environment, viewed his role as one of "survival" rather than progress. His competitor's company was thriving, implementing strategies that fostered employee development. The mounting pressure led him to seek quick fixes instead of sustainable solutions. Through coaching, he identified his strengths and committed to team growth. This shift enabled him to make bolder, more innovative decisions, elevating team performance and positioning his unit as a key driver of organizational success. His team transitioned from merely completing tasks to continuously seeking improvement and innovation.

A third client, a manager in a large organization, operated

reactively, consumed by daily issues, leaving no time for personal or career growth. He constantly felt off track. During a strategic session, he was assigned to lead a high-stakes project with a cross-departmental team. Doubt crept in: "Am I truly ready for this?" However, reflecting on past successes in our coaching session reignited his confidence. He began to see the project as an opportunity for growth. The journey was tough—navigating diverse perspectives, strategic shifts, and executive pressure—but coaching helped him approach challenges creatively. As the project advanced, so did his leadership skills and ability to navigate complex dynamics. Ultimately, the project became a career-defining success, fostering both professional and personal growth. His team's productivity soared, and the organizational culture improved. He was no longer just a project manager but a transformational leader. Through coaching, he achieved both personal and professional success, empowering others to follow a similar path and fostering a culture of growth within the company.

These examples clearly demonstrate that resilience alone cannot lead to true employee flourishing. Only when employees recognize their strengths and gain confidence in their decision-making can they transform from resilience to flourishing. This transformation not only boosts productivity and innovation but also turns employees into influential forces within organizations, enabling them to thrive in successful companies. This is why organizations focus on employee flourishing.

What's Your Next Step?

You are more than an employee; you are a brand, an asset, and a potential influencer. Your growth benefits both you and your organization. Recognizing your potential isn't enough—you must take proactive steps toward personal and professional development.

- **Are You Flourishing or Just Enduring?** Ask yourself honestly: Are you merely surviving or actively growing?
- **What's the First Step toward Growth?** Start by clarifying your goals. What skills do you need to advance?
- **How Does Coaching Elevate Your Career?** Coaching provides guidance on your path to flourishing.

Flourishing in Action: Critical Thinking and Coaching Exercises

1. Future Self Email – "Your Best Self in a Year"

- **Objective:** Visualize growth and take ownership of your journey; shape your career and impact your organization in meaningful ways.

Write an email to yourself, dated one year from today, imagining that you have flourished in your role. Consider your progress as an employee, a team member, or a department manager. Be specific about your achievements and the mindset shifts that have driven your success.

- **Key Milestones:** What professional goals have you reached? Have you led successful projects, improved key skills, or contributed to your team's success in a meaningful way?
- **Handling Challenges:** How do you approach obstacles differently now? What strategies have you developed to navigate uncertainty and change?
- **Effective Habits:** What new routines or behaviors have helped you become more efficient, resilient, or influential within your team?
- **Guidance from Your Future Self:** If your future self could advise you today, what insights would they share? What should you start, stop, or continue doing to reach your full potential?

Take a few moments to craft this email as if your future self were speaking to you. Save it, schedule it to be sent a year from now, or revisit it periodically to track your progress.

2. "What If" Challenge – Expanding Your Comfort Zone

- **Objective:** Challenge assumptions and build adaptability.

Answer these questions in writing:

What if you lost your job tomorrow? How prepared are you?

What if you had to lead unexpectedly? What strengths and gaps would you address?

What if failure weren't an option? What bold decision would you make today?

3. The "Unspoken Assumptions" Test

- **Objective:** Challenge limiting beliefs.

Identify an assumption holding you back:

- "I can't ask for a promotion because..."
- "I avoid speaking up because..."
- "I don't take risks because..."
- "I can't change my life because..."

Challenge it:

- Is this always true?
- What's the worst that could happen if you did the opposite?
- What step can you take this week to challenge this belief?

4. The Flourishing Scorecard

- **Objective:** Assess well-being using the PERMA model.

Rate yourself (1-10) in these five areas:

- **Positive Emotions:** Joy, gratitude, optimism
- **Engagement:** Deep involvement in meaningful activities
- **Relationships:** Supportive connections
- **Meaning:** Strong sense of purpose
- **Accomplishment:** Progress toward goals

Reflection: Which area scored the lowest? What action can you take this month to improve it?

5. The "90-Day Growth Experiment"

- **Objective:** Shift from passive survival to intentional flourishing.

Choose one growth area for the next 90 days (leadership, communication, decision-making, stress management, health, confidence, work-life balance, emotional intelligence).

- **Step 1:** Identify a small, consistent habit to support growth.
- **Step 2:** Anticipate a challenge and plan to overcome it.
- **Step 3:** Find an accountability partner (mentor, colleague, friend).

6. The "Invisible Impact" Reflection – Your Legacy

- **Objective:** Recognize your deeper impact beyond daily routines.

Answer these honestly:

- If you left your company today, how would you be remembered?
- What lasting impact are you making?
- What kind of mentor or leader do you aspire to be?
- What one action can you take this week to strengthen your legacy?

Use these insights and exercises to challenge assumptions,

unlock potential, and take intentional steps toward a flourishing life—both personally and professionally.

Now ask yourself: What bold action can you take today to move from merely surviving to truly flourishing?

Thank you for joining me in this chapter. For a free step-by-step guide, "Thriving in Your Career and Life: Practical Strategies for Growth," visit www.mohsenkhakicoaching.com (Articles section). If you're interested in working directly with me as your coach, send a request to mohsenkhakicoaching@yahoo.com or visit the "Services/Request Coaching Sessions" section on my website.

From Surviving to Thriving
A Coaching Guide to Flourishing at Work and Beyond

About the Author

Mohsen Khaki is an author, an internationally certified professional coach by the International Coaching Federation (ICF), and a branding specialist. He began his professional journey at the age of eighteen by teaching English. Changes in his career path started in the early years when he decided to switch to teaching English after graduating from university with a degree in mechanical engineering. The initial failure in his entrepreneurial journey gave Mohsen a profound perspective on the challenges and opportunities for strengthening his brand. With over two decades of experience in language teaching and educational consulting, Mohsen built a strong reputation in preparing students for international exams, especially IELTS, through thousands of impactful workshops. His deep understanding of human learning, communication, and motivation naturally sparked a desire to create greater value beyond the classroom. This passion led him to explore the fields of business management, marketing and sales, branding, and psychology. Eventually, he pursued specialized international coaching programs, integrating his teaching expertise with coaching methodologies to support business development and personal transformation.

He is now active as a successful professional coach at the global level and, relying on the experience of conducting thousands of hours of specialized coaching and hundreds of international consultations, he assists business owners, leaders, and organization managers in creating a sustainable leadership framework, transformative action plan, agile strategy, growth mindset, and an innovative culture in business and increasing team productivity. In addition, he has designed and implemented numerous programs and workshops aimed at identifying and nurturing individual and professional talents. In this way, he helps people, including organization employees, to advance their personal and professional paths in the best possible way by identifying their strengths. Mohsen is passionate about learning, studying, his own personal growth and that of others, and has a keen interest in sports, travel, and music.

You can contact him in the following ways:

For coaching:

- www.mohsenkhakicoaching.com,
- mohsenkhakicoaching@yahoo.com,
- mohsenkhakicoaching.

For IELTS:

- www.mohsenkhaki-ielts.com,
- ieltskhaki@gmail.com,
- IELTS Khaki.

Shining in the Heart of Darkness
Navigating a Foggy Path When Only Your Inner Light Illuminates the Way

Mohammad Mehri

Shining in the Heart of Darkness
Navigating a Foggy Path When Only Your Inner Light Illuminates the Way

Mohammad Mehri
Flight Engineer, Mental Clarity Coach

Like a Rainbow

Some memories are so beautiful they stay with you forever, unforgettable no matter how much time goes by. I remember a sunny day in a large park, with a gentle breeze blowing. The shade of the tall trees, like a protective umbrella, sheltered me sitting on the ground. It was a natural blessing. I watched people pass through the park, individuals hurrying toward their destinations. Each of them had their own story; they likely had jobs and were contemplating the path they had traveled in life to get to where they were today. Were they in their ideal positions? Were they satisfied with their careers?

Lost in these thoughts, the sound of children playing captured my attention. They enjoyed playing with my pinwheels for free, as long as they didn't damage them. This was an arrangement I had with the children of nearby vendors. Whenever the wind blew, the pinwheels would spin, creating a magnificent display, like a rainbow.

Yes, I was the pinwheel vendor in the park. After a major bankruptcy, this was the only work I could do to cover my university expenses. It was very challenging for me at first, but gradually it turned into a very enjoyable experience. It was my first time selling directly to people.

However, one question constantly occupied my mind—a question I couldn't forget and for which I had no answer: "What have I come into this world to do?"

This fragment of my memories is a piece of my existence. Now, I am a coach, an author, and also a flight engineer. I have always searched for my own path in life, employing various methods to discover what that path was. For a long time, I felt as if I were walking along a foggy path, unable to see the destination. But sometimes, having at least one powerful question can serve as a small light for taking the next steps. This was the question that accompanied me throughout my entire journey: "What have I come into this world to do?"

Now that I look back, I realize that the path I have traveled thus far is much more exciting to me than the road that lies ahead. I always thought the final destination had to be completely clear and obvious, and that I just had to do my best to reach that goal. It took me a long time to understand that the real joy of life is in the journey itself, with all its bitterness, memories, and challenges. Along the way, I faced many questions, ambiguities, and fears:

"Am I on the right path?" "What if I make a mistake?" "What if I have to go back and start from scratch?"

I struggled to understand why so many things happened.

Sometimes this foggy path feels endless, and only specific signs can, like a candle in the darkness of a room, create a glow of heartfelt certainty that we are on the right track—signs that can keep the buds of hope for the future alive in our hearts.

Hearing the Whisper of Love When Fear Screams

During my first days in the park, I made no sales. People simply walked by, paying no attention to me. Of course, I avoided their gaze as well. I was very introverted, even afraid of someone approaching me to ask for the price. The concept of selling had always been frightening to me. Asking others to pay me money felt very difficult. I tried various methods to attract people's attention and make a sale. For example, one time I tied several pinwheels to trees in different parts of the park to make them more visible, which, of course, drew opposition from the park guard. Other attempts also ended in failure.

My biggest fear was that the pinwheels wouldn't sell. I was also worried that if I let the kids in the park play with them, they might get damaged, leaving me with nothing left to sell. At the peak of my fear and anxiety, I chose to listen to the whisper of love over the scream of fear inside me, a decision that brought a sense of peace to my life. I remember my first sale, which happened when I decided to let children who couldn't afford to buy from me play with the pinwheels. After that, those same children became my product's advertisers, leading to sales I had never even dreamed of. In that moment, I recalled my mother's words from my childhood: "When you help clear the road for others, God smooths the way for you."

By giving the gift of playing with pinwheels to those children, I was rewarded soon after. This became my guiding principle during my most successful sales experiences.

Reveal Your Treasures Through the Eyes of Others

I supported my university expenses by street vending in the park. The reference books for my specialized field of study were expensive, and I also needed to cover personal expenses and tuition. Initially, I found the university lessons manageable, but as I progressed, the subjects became increasingly challenging. While I had a good aptitude for learning, many of my classmates struggled to grasp the material. This sparked an idea in me. Since I didn't have enough time outside of university to review my lessons, I decided to teach the same material to my classmates during our breaks. I truly enjoyed this, especially seeing how easily I could convey the concepts to them.

One day, while I was drinking coffee in the university café, a classmate approached me, and we started talking. He said, "You have a real talent for teaching and explaining things!" He then asked me to tutor him and a few others privately for a fee to help them prepare for the final exams. I felt both happy and surprised. I replied, "Why don't you ask the professor to do it?" knowing that professors often welcomed such arrangements.

He responded, "When the professor teaches, we don't

understand much, but when you explain it to us, we get it easily." This feedback was a crucial realization for me—something I might not have recognized on my own. The pleasure of hearing this was ten times greater than the joy I felt from receiving money.

It was there that I realized we often possess assets within us that we are unaware of, and feedback from others can be incredibly helpful. This became one of the most significant indicators for finding the right path in my life: the treasure chests within us, which can only be seen through the eyes of others.

Where Time Stands Still: Discovering Flow Through Connection

As I continued teaching at the university, I, an introverted person, soon made many friends. Gradually, my connection with them deepened, and we formed a group that communicated beyond university matters and engaged in recreational activities together. For someone like me, with a very small circle of friends, this was immensely enjoyable and allowed me to cultivate closer relationships. Over time, I became familiar with many of their lives. During our conversations, I noticed many admirable qualities in their characters, and eventually, I realized I could easily identify each person's strengths. This discovery excited me, and I pursued it with enthusiasm. Every interaction confirmed my ability to see people's talents and strengths.

Giving them feedback on these strengths soon led me to speak more frequently within this group, to the point where I lost track of time whenever I engaged with them. Additionally, I received positive feedback afterward. Although our conversations often lasted a long time, I shared my thoughts with great excitement and passion. I realized that "work you do with such enthusiasm that you lose track of time is a sign it is one of your inner treasures."

Don't Run from the Venomous Snake; Embrace It!

Making many friends at the university, building close relationships, and participating in group activities significantly boosted my self-confidence. I had always struggled to connect with others, but at university, the circumstances allowed me to navigate a process of getting to know people that proved very beneficial. I felt comfortable in a large group and communicated easily with its members. They trusted me, and I received positive energy from them. As we gradually approached the end of our university studies, I, along with one of my close friends, chose a project for our thesis that involved simulating the voice communication between an aircraft and the control tower on a specific frequency. By incorporating a new system, we enabled the aircraft to communicate via text chat as well. This was achieved with significantly lower energy consumption than under normal conditions, which is crucial for a pilot during an emergency. In situations where the aircraft's power was completely cut off, this system could operate using a small battery and had an effective range of several kilometers.

Our practical project performed very well in the initial tests and was submitted to another university that was collecting similar projects from all participating institutions. It was decided that I would present our work to a large audience of professors and students. This is where a wave of fear washed over me. While I spoke comfortably among my friends, the thought of addressing such an audience terrified me. My teammate, who had worked on the project with me, was completely unwilling to present. Ultimately, at the insistence of my supervising professor, I decided to take on the task myself. I was convinced it wouldn't go well and braced myself for possible ridicule. But I didn't have much of a choice — as the university's representative, it was my responsibility to go through with it.

The day of the presentation arrived. My palms were sweaty, and my knees were trembling. As I stood behind the microphone and my eyes scanned the audience, terror enveloped me. For a moment, I completely forgot why I was there and what I was supposed to discuss. I lacked experience speaking in such settings, which added to my anxiety. I took a few deep breaths and began. The tremor in my voice was quite noticeable, and I felt ashamed of it.

After a short while, one of the attendees raised their hand to ask a question. I had braced myself for something like, "Wasn't there anyone better than you to explain this?" but the question asked was: "I was wondering how you concluded that you could lower energy consumption so much with this method?"

I stared at the person as if I couldn't hear them. They repeated their question because I had fallen silent. After a few moments, I regained my composure and began explaining the operational protocol that had helped us achieve significant energy reduction. A few others asked questions, and I answered more comfortably than before, no longer feeling my legs shaking.

After my presentation, it was a short break, and those who had asked questions approached me. They expressed that our work was very interesting and, more importantly, remarked, "You presented the project very well and were very confident!"

Initially, I felt as if they were mocking me, but as the conversation continued, I realized they were entirely sincere. How could I possibly do well — with sweaty palms, shaky legs, and a trembling voice I could clearly hear myself? And yet... how had they not noticed?

In that moment, a profound truth was revealed to me. The project was no longer my focus; instead, I understood that all this fear was an illusion I had created, visible only to me. My fear resembled an imaginary picture I had constructed, which did not exist in the external world and vanished when I confronted the situation.

This fear served as a signpost for speaking to a larger crowd—a talent that required reminding. And the messenger of this lesson was a fearsome snake. That day, I realized the snake I feared wasn't there to harm me—it came to awaken a strength I never knew I had.

It Bothers You Until You Get Its Message

Having an excellent thesis, strong academic record, and a successful job interview led me to immediately start working as a flight engineer at the country's top airline. I was very happy to find myself in such a situation—holding a position that many people dream of. Days passed, and I learned more about airplanes and how systems function in different aircraft models. This was immensely enjoyable for me, and I was progressing rapidly.

We had specific, standardized procedures for troubleshooting potential aircraft problems. However, over time, the work became difficult and monotonous for me, losing the pleasure it once brought. We would see a sign and take the necessary action, but that was insufficient for me. In fact, it became very annoying and felt unappealing because I felt like a robot.

I was doing the tasks that needed to be done and were correct, but I didn't have enough personal reason behind them. So, I decided to fully understand the processes we were following rather than just going through the motions. My colleagues found it unusual that I was putting in extra effort. I also found their approach peculiar; I often wondered why they never questioned the reasons behind their tasks.

As time passed, I gained a clearer understanding of the processes and developed a strong sense of them. Even when I was on the plane or flying, I would simulate in my mind which computer was communicating with which system and what was happening at that moment. Once I mastered the processes, an important issue caught my attention: I was able to easily diagnose errors within a system, which I found intriguing. One day, I reflected on my university experience and realized that I possessed a similar ability to identify systemic errors in people's approaches, understanding where they were going wrong and why they weren't achieving their desired goals.

This realization stemmed from a single factor. The aspect that initially frustrated me became a sign that highlighted an important skill: the ability to identify errors within a system.

Today, as I stand in the role of a Mental Clarity Coach, I am still on my journey. I attribute my progress to the signs and messages I have received from the language of the universe: Attention to the love within, feedback from those around you, a passion that transcends time, the fears you have embraced, and the annoyances seeking your attention.

Shining in the Heart of Darkness

Navigating a Foggy Path When Only Your Inner Light Illuminates the Way

About the Author

Mohammad Mehri is a Flight Engineer and a Mental Clarity Coach. He began his career in aviation engineering, a field where precision, observation, and impartial analysis are essential. After years of experience in the aviation industry, Mohammad made an important discovery: many of life's flights falter in the human mind long before they ever crash in the sky. With this insight, he embarked on a new journey into personal development and coaching.

Today, with the same precision he applies as a flight engineer, Mohammad Mehri helps individuals re-evaluate their mental maps, identify hidden obstacles, and design a clear and effective path to success.

He is also an author of the book *Coaching Insights*, published on Amazon. This book combines the science, art, and philosophy of coaching, narrating a journey from the hard realities of life to the hopeful horizons of possibility.

Mohammad believes that coaching, like flight engineering, is not merely about direct guidance but about fostering growth and facilitating self-leadership in others. Through his "Mental Clarity Coaching" method, he helps people find their clear path amidst chaos and countless choices, empowering them to move forward with confidence.

For those ready to embark on a new journey in their lives, Mohammad is not just a coach but a thought partner and an architect of inner transformation.

Connect with the Author:

⊙ Mohamadmehri.coach
⊕ Mohamadmehri.coach
✉ Mohamadmehri.coach@gmail.com
☎ (+98) 935 898 9891

That Which You Dread Is Where You're Led

Marjan Shams

That Which You Dread Is Where You're Led

Marjan Shams

Researcher, Professional Coach and Trainer in Personal Development and Leadership, Founder of the Academy of Flourishing and Leadership

What Is Growing in the Silence of Your Mind?

In a world filled with economic, social, and environmental changes and instabilities, it's natural to sometimes feel doubt, worry, and even fear. The challenges that arise can often seem so vast that we feel overwhelmed and incapable of confronting them. In such an unstable and fast-paced environment, fears like the fear of the future, failure, change, or judgment from others can take root in our hearts.

But are these fears always our enemy, as they seem?

Rumi, with a profound perspective, answers this question in a simple yet meaningful verse: **"Whatever you tremble for, know that you are worth that much."**[1]

Fears guide you toward what is important and valuable to you. Where fear exists, there lies the seed of your growth.

Fear is neither an obstacle to overcome nor a voice to silence;

---

1. *Divan-e Shams-e Tabrizi* (The Collected Poems of Shams), a major work by the 13th-century Persian poet and mystic Jalaluddin Rumi. Ghazal 609 explores the theme of inner truth and emotional resonance.

it is an invitation to a deeper understanding of ourselves and the discovery of hidden paths within. It beckons us to move forward, even with trembling knees, on a journey that makes us feel more alive.

Fears Are Smaller Than You Imagine!

The fears you face are indicators of the values that matter to you. The more valuable something is, the greater the fear of losing it or failing to achieve it. For example, the fear of failing in a work project might signal your desire for progress and financial security, while the fear of judgment from others might reflect your need for acceptance, belonging, and recognition.

It can be said that fear is neither your enemy nor your impediment; rather, it is a guide. Fear indicates that something in your life is important to you and may be under threat. This is precisely the moment to use as a catalyst for greater effort.

Most fears generated by our minds never materialize in reality, and even the few that do are not as bad as we anticipated. So perhaps each time you feel fear, instead of fleeing from it, you should ask yourself: "What inner value is this fear expressing?"

Fears Are the Seed of Flourishing in the Soil of the Unknown

Many individuals who have achieved great success initially faced considerable fear and doubt, but they transformed these fears into opportunities for learning and growth. One of the most crucial steps in this transformation is shifting your perspective.

Fear typically arises from the unknown and new situations. However, if you view these situations as opportunities for learning and growth, fear can transform into motivation. The fear of failure can be an opportunity to learn from mistakes and improve skills, while the fear of change can foster greater flexibility in the face of new circumstances.

By changing your perspective, you can utilize fear as a driving force. For example, rather than fearing a career change, you can see it as an opportunity to acquire new skills or advance in your professional journey. Similarly, the fear of failure can compel you to exert more effort and enter the arena with greater preparation.

Dancing with Shadows

Personal flourishing in today's world is not a simple, linear process. It begins not on a direct path, but in moments of pause and doubt, and within the heart of uncertainty.

Every step we take today is accompanied by the sound of fear's shadows—a fear that sometimes disperses like smoke in the air and at other times rises like a wave from the depths of the sea. But why do we flee from or turn our backs on our fears? In reality, it is not fear that threatens us, but our reaction to it. Christopher Paolini, the American author, states in *The Inheritance Cycle* that fear has a large shadow, but by itself, it is small and powerless.

Flourishing in today's world involves understanding this truth: that fear is a part of our being we should not run from, but rather embrace. Only then can we harness fear to drive progress and foster awareness. This is a dance—a dance between shadow and light. Be free and step forward, for every fear you overcome dispels a shadow from your past and allows the light of your future to shine.

A Shadow That Illuminates the Path!

Fear often appears on our life's path with an obscure and dark face. However, if we pause for a moment and examine it, we will see that it is merely a shadow of something we have not yet achieved—something that can serve as a gateway to flourishing. If we choose to view fear not as an obstacle but as a sign of awareness, our perspective will shift dramatically.

Below, I will share three scientific approaches—tools that can help us use fear as an opportunity to shine brighter as we move forward.

Growth Mindset: Fear Is an Invitation to Learn!

Carol Dweck, a prominent psychologist, categorizes human mindsets into two types: fixed mindset and growth mindset.[1]

A fixed mindset, which believes "I am who I am," tends to

---

1. Dweck, C. (2016). What having a growth mindset actually means. *Harvard Business Review*.

retreat in the face of the fear of failure. In contrast, a growth mindset, which embraces the idea that "I can grow," plants the seed of learning within fear.

A growth mindset allows us to view the fear of new situations, mistakes, and failures not as threats, but as exercises to strengthen our inner growth.

Emotional Intelligence: If You Know Fear, You Tame It!

Fear often arises not from external dangers but from our internal perceptions. Emotional intelligence is the ability to recognize and embrace our emotions. For instance, if you fear public speaking, it might stem from a fear of judgment or rejection. However, when you understand the root of that emotion, you can channel it instead of hiding from it.

Our brains crave certainty; they always want to know what happens next. Yet, life is often too foggy to predict with precision. Uncertainty management involves accepting that not everything needs to be clear, allowing us to move forward with faith.

Beyond Fear: A New Beginning

We now understand that fear is not an enemy meant to stop us, but rather a guide for a new beginning. We simply need to view it from a different perspective. This shift requires practice and, more importantly, a supportive companion who consciously encourages us on our path to progress.

Fear in the Mirror of Coaching: Finding Light in the Shadows Within

Fear has the greatest power when it is invisible, much like shadows that shrink when illuminated. The first step in the coaching process is to help individuals identify and name their fears. Is it a fear of failure, a fear of being ignored, or perhaps a fear of success and the responsibilities that accompany it?

In a session with Elnaz, one of my clients, it became clear that what held her back was the fear of being overlooked, not the fear of failure. This discovery marked the beginning of her inner liberation: once she recognized what frightened her, she no longer felt the need to hide. Elnaz found her path and took action.

Dancing in the Shadows of Awareness: Uncovering Fear's Message Through Coaching

Many studies have been conducted on the acceptance of fear. These studies show that fears can sometimes be a sign of hidden opportunities for personal and professional growth.[1] If you look at your fear from a different perspective, you will see that it is not a threat to you, but rather a path to discovering new aspects of yourself.

Coaching can facilitate this shift in perspective. By asking questions such as "What is hidden within this fear?" or

---

1. Riepenhausen, A., et al. (2022). Positive cognitive reappraisal in stress resilience, mental health, and well-being: A comprehensive systematic review. *Emotion Review, 14*(4).

"How can you use this fear for your personal growth?", fear transforms from an obstacle into an opportunity for discovering and strengthening new qualities and skills.

A study published in 2020 shows that individuals who embrace their fear in decision-making as part of the learning process perform up to 35% better when facing complex challenges and difficult decisions.[1]

After reviewing her fears, Elnaz realized that her concerns about large projects stemmed from their high importance. She decided that instead of avoiding these fears, she would view them as signs of her growth path and move forward step by step. Ultimately, Elnaz communicated with her team with greater courage and pursued her projects with more confidence.

Starting Coaching in Moments of Fear: Transforming Ambiguity into Action

When faced with a large project or goal, our minds naturally perceive it as a threat. However, if we divide that perceived threat into smaller, manageable steps, we will no longer fear it.

The SMART model[2] is specifically designed for such situations. By clearly defining goals and breaking them down into smaller parts, this model can transform fear into an

---

1. Wake, S., et al. (2020). The influence of fear on risk taking: A meta-analysis. *Cognition and Emotion*.
2. In the SMART model, a goal should have five key characteristics: it must be **Specific**, **Measurable**, **Achievable**, **Relevant** to our values and priorities, and **Time-bound** with a clear deadline.

opportunity for action. Elnaz divided her large and challenging project into small, manageable steps. She initially chose to send just one important email to her colleagues. This small step boosted her confidence, enabling her to tackle the rest of the project with greater courage.

Coaching in Silence: Inner Peace, Conscious Steps

A mind entangled in anxiety cannot function effectively. When overwhelmed by worries, conflicting thoughts, and stress, our ability to make decisions and take action diminishes. In such circumstances, even when we intend to take significant steps, we struggle to focus and move forward.

In coaching, we help individuals calm their minds and be present in the moment. One of the most effective tools for this purpose is mind-calming techniques. These tools enhance our self-control when facing challenges and psychological pressures. Techniques such as focusing on conscious breathing and enhancing self-awareness enable us to break free from anxiety and proceed more courageously along our path.

I encourage my clients to spend a few minutes alone before important meetings or challenging tasks, focusing on their breath and their presence in the moment. This practice helps them escape the trap of scattered thoughts and anxiety, preparing their minds for more conscious decisions. Research has shown that consistent practice of increasing self-awareness and mind control can alter the brain's structure, allowing individuals to respond better to negative emotions, especially anxiety and fear. These practices gradually strengthen decision-making abilities, enhance concentration, and improve overall quality of life.

Elnaz initially struggled with the pressures and anxieties related to significant projects, but after coaching and learning mind-calming techniques, she dedicated just a few minutes to breathing and being present before important meetings or sensitive decisions. This simple change yielded extraordinary results. Remarkably, she improved her performance and made better decisions with a calm and focused mind.

Mind-calming not only reduces anxiety but also strengthens decision-making abilities and enhances performance. This process helps clients navigate their journeys calmly and with greater awareness amid mental storms, guiding them toward their goals.

Coaching Through Conscious Presence: a Bridge from Loneliness to Connection

No one should fight their fears alone. Even the bravest individuals have days when they need support—a hand to hold, a look that understands, a voice that says, "You are not alone."

Social support is not merely the presence of others, but the quality of that presence, allowing you to be authentic. Support groups—whether formal (such as coaching groups, personal growth workshops, or empathetic work teams) or informal (like real friends, family, or a coach)—can play a vital role in overcoming fears.

Positive psychologists believe that the feeling of belonging is one of the fundamental needs of the human psyche. Individuals who are part of strong support networks not only demonstrate greater resilience to challenges but also increase their likelihood of success in pursuing long-term goals. Hearing others' stories, empathizing with them, and drawing inspiration from their successes and setbacks provide the courage to move forward. In group conversations, sparks of awareness often ignite: someone who didn't know you suddenly illuminates a light in your mind with a simple sentence.

In group coaching, Elnaz realized she wasn't alone. She discovered that others shared similar fears and came to understand that fear is not a personal weakness but a part of the human experience. This awareness unleashed a force within her—a force born from a sense of belonging. Elnaz no longer viewed herself as isolated but as part of a shared journey.

Leading from Within: Coaching for Fear, Acceptance, and Growth

Accepting fear, especially in today's fast-paced world where change and challenges are constant, is difficult for many. The coaching process helps individuals confront their fears, understand them, and instead of fleeing, find a way to effectively address them. One of the main methods coaching employs to accept fear is creating awareness. The coach, through insightful questions, invites the individual to examine and analyze their fears. These questions encourage the individual to view their fears from a different perspective. The coaching process allows individuals to coexist with their fears and continue moving forward even in the face of their greatest challenges.

In her coaching sessions, Elnaz came to view her fears as part of her journey rather than its end. She learned that her fears carried a message; by listening to them, she was able to use them to make progress. Essentially, Elnaz discovered that instead of running from her fears, she could use them as a starting point for change. Coaching helped Elnaz transform her fears from a large, impassable fortress into a bridge. She realized that despite her fears, she could still bravely take steps forward on her growth path.

When Awareness Awakens Through Coaching

In the coaching journey, when an individual achieves sufficient self-awareness and clarity, they enter a phase called "action orientation." In this phase, the individual no longer settles for limited self-knowledge and understanding of their environment. Instead, they reach a point where they are ready to translate this knowledge into action, taking targeted and calculated steps. One of the most important actions in this phase is precise planning and the use of advanced analytical tools. Scientific research has shown that coaching can significantly impact individuals' action orientation; the performance level of the vast majority of participants in coaching sessions increases. These individuals not only enhance their professional performance but also take more effective actions in their personal lives.[1]

The GROW model[2], used in many coaching processes, can help individuals set specific goals at each stage of their journey and design effective implementation strategies.

Additionally, techniques such as SWOT[3] and SMART directly contribute to improving individuals' action orientation.

To move toward action orientation, it is sometimes necessary to utilize various other tools. One such tool is Transactional Analysis, which helps individuals better understand their communication and make informed decisions based on that understanding.

Elnaz achieved astonishing results using the SWOT model. She identified her strengths, including strong communication skills and a high ability to work in teams. Aware of her weaknesses, such as a lack of confidence in making major decisions, she sought solutions to strengthen these areas. She also effectively identified opportunities in new projects and managed existing threats.

---

1. Jones, R., & Woods, S. (2016). The effectiveness of workplace coaching: A meta-analysis of learning and performance outcomes from coaching. *Journal of Occupational and Organizational Psychology*.
2. The GROW model is an acronym representing four stages: **Goal**, **Reality**, **Obstacles**, and **Way Forward**. This coaching framework helps individuals define their objectives and develop actionable plans to achieve them.
3. SWOT analysis—an acronym for **Strengths**, **Weaknesses**, **Opportunities**, and **Threats**—serves as a powerful tool in coaching, guiding individuals toward deeper self-awareness and effective strategic planning.

Concluding Remarks: Walking Toward the Light Within

Fear, like a shadow standing before light, appears more powerful in moments of darkness. However, when you step onto the path, you realize that the shadow is merely part of the interplay between light and darkness. Fear is neither our enemy nor something to flee from; instead, it is a force that invites us to confront the unseen aspects of ourselves.

Seek your own light. Even when the sky is cloudy, your inner sun is always ready to rise.

That Which You Dread Is Where You're Led

About the Author

Marjan Shams holds official certification from the International Coaching Federation (ICF), a Master of Business Administration (MBA), and expertise in transactional analysis, personality profiling, and behavioral etiquette. She began her coaching journey with a deep and humane perspective, having had the honor of completing a transformative course with Dr. Shahab Anari. Marjan continues to learn with passion and enthusiasm. Beyond her degrees and skills, it is the path she has walked—a journey both inward and outward toward a deeper understanding of humanity, the roots of its behaviors, and its capacity for inner transformation.

Marjan, the multi-faceted woman in this narrative, is both a mother and a wife. Amidst her family life, she is a dedicated teacher who illuminates the light of learning in the darkest corners of doubt.

Her interests in philosophy, psychology, yoga, and mindfulness have transformed her soul into a garden rich with pure questions and awakening silences. Her love for playing the piano and horseback riding has taught her that life is a blend of order, rhythm, and liberation.

She believes that humans are not dormant suns, but rather lights sometimes obscured by clouds of dust.

For Marjan, coaching is not merely a skill; it is an invitation to return to oneself, to hear the inner voice, and to initiate a new movement from the heart of awareness.

Her mission is to create a space for conscious transformation—a place where individuals can reclaim their authentic selves, organizations can be revitalized with their human spirit, and development becomes an integral part of our daily lives rather than just a management term.

Marjan serves as a bridge between self-knowledge and effectiveness, between introspection and professional action, and between the dream of growth and the tangible realities of life.

Contact the Author:

✉ marjanshams965@gmail.com
🌐 www.marjanshams.com
📷 Marjanshams

The Star I Couldn't Find in the Sky
From Cosmic Questions to Inner Light: A Journey toward Flourishing

Dr. Alireza Talebian

The Star I Couldn't Find in the Sky
From Cosmic Questions to Inner Light: A Journey toward Flourishing

Dr. Alireza Talebian
Researcher, Flourishing Coach, and High-Performance Master Trainer, Founder of the Innerstellar Group

Scene One: The Seed Planted Beneath the Plum Trees!

With my wife's tweezers, I plucked the last white hair that was showing off on my face, and carefully hid my gray hair under my old black hat. That day, my wife couldn't pick up the boys from school, and I had to go after them. Since returning from the trip to Japan, this was my second time picking them up. I was ready to leave when the sound of two alarms, spaced slightly apart, interrupted my thoughts; the first was a reminder on my phone: it was prompting me to send a research code to a colleague so he could use it for his new project. The second was the doorbell at home: the kids had come home on their own. Relieved that I wouldn't have to go out, I quickly settled behind my laptop, refined the latest version of the code, and prepared it to send to my colleague.

As I was going to click the send email button, familiar questions surfaced: "Why does sending a code to your colleagues bring you joy, yet picking up your sons fills you with anxiety? Where does your struggle lie? What have you lost? Wasn't your true happiness once entwined with the sound of your children's laughter? What is it that truly brings joy to your family and your sons?" I knew precisely where these questions had taken root—their seeds had been planted in me thirteen days earlier, thousands of kilometers away.

Thirteen days earlier, invited by the Yukawa Institute, I arrived at Kyoto University in Japan. Atabak, an Iranian-born student raised in Sweden, would occasionally take me on tours around the city of Kyoto. On one such outing, I borrowed a bicycle from my kind supervisor, Professor Shinji Mukohyama, and we pedaled to Kitano Tenmangū Shrine, revered for wisdom and knowledge, where students pray for academic success.

It was winter, and the plum trees had painted a mesmerizing scene around the temple in the absence of cherry blossoms. Amid the beauty, something felt subtly off. As Atabak took photos, I murmured, "I wish my children were here. They'd love this, and I'd love seeing their joy." He lowered his camera and replied, "Honestly, if I were them, I wouldn't want my father to sacrifice his life just for us." His words did not sit well with me at first. "Maybe," I said, "but I don't think so. There are aspects of life that you don't know about." Atabak said nothing, but his words were like a seed planted in the depths of my mind, and it seemed I built a dam out of fear to prevent watering that seed of thought. I don't know what the real source of this fear was; perhaps I was afraid of disrupting the relative peace of my job and family. However,

I was unaware that this seed could find its own way without needing fertile soil or waiting for rain.

Upon returning to Tehran, though spring hadn't arrived, I could already sense the seed within me stirring—seeking light, eager to emerge—yet I consciously chose to ignore it. My feelings toward it were like those of a mother upset with her child, feigning indifference while secretly watching every move. Two days after returning, I took advantage of some post-trip leave and picked up my sons from school. Standing near the newly-painted janitor's room, many parents were waiting for their children. I saw my sons from afar and called them, and we walked home together. Yet I didn't see the joy I'd hoped for in their eyes. At home, as I washed my hands and face, I overheard my son telling his mother, "Can Dad stop picking me up? He's really old! My friends' fathers are much younger!" I couldn't pretend not to hear. The cracks on the dam were getting bigger and deeper, and I couldn't stop the flow of water. And so, the seed planted beneath the plum trees of the shrine of wisdom and knowledge began to sprout, bloom, and with its pollination, perfumed my entire being. Its trunk, thickening like a legendary beanstalk, suddenly grew and pulled me out from beneath the heavy weight of mud. Although I was experiencing seemingly painful moments, I had a strange sense of lightness. Like a butterfly chasing the light, I rode the branches of that plum tree, moving toward a light of hope that could reshape my future forever. From that height, I became aware of my behaviors and thoughts, and could analyze and understand myself more than before.

After a while, I was invited on another research trip to the Bernoulli Center for Fundamental Studies *located on the EPFL campus in Lausanne*, Switzerland. For this trip, I chose clothes in yellow and red, leaving behind my simple black hat. I changed my facial appearance: a neatly trimmed professor-style beard, supported by an even fuller mustache. Up close, one could easily detect the presence of white hairs on my face, but the predominance of black in the mustache had found a good harmony with the uniform black eyebrows and yellow-green glasses. Typically, I wasn't one for taking pictures, but this time was different—I wandered through the city, capturing moments in photographs. Atabak's words echoed in my mind, urging me to enjoy the beauty around me. As I sent my pictures to my family, my homesickness lessened. I had realized that when I am happy here, they are happier.

Upon my return, I continued wearing the same clothes at the School of Astronomy (SoA) at the Institute for Research in Fundamental Sciences (IPM). My colleagues, who had known me for five years, assumed that my new style was due to the trip to Switzerland. But the truth was, everything had begun when my sons watered the seed planted beneath the plum trees.

Scene Two: Between Earth and Cosmos

It was Arbor Day, and I found myself in Larak Garden, the largest property of the Institute for Research in Fundamental Sciences, planting saplings alongside other members. With a friend's help, I planted my sapling and passed the shovel. Yet, my thoughts lingered on my computer back in the office, simulating and calculating gravitational waves from the early universe. Nearly all the PhD students, postdocs, and faculty gathered to mark the day by planting trees, hoping to leave a better Earth for future generations. With a gentle smile, I moved to join the group photo when my hand brushed a tree branch. The sting transported me back sixty-seven months, to a time when sweat and tears soaked the blister on my hand that had just burst, sweat from the desert sun and tears of joy from receiving the news that a credible international journal had accepted our paper for publication. I was elated knowing I could finally defend my dissertation and leave life in remote villages. If all went well, I would join researchers running galaxy or black hole collision simulations on advanced computers, unveiling the beauty of the cosmos.

Believing even a tiny room, with just a worn-out chair and internet access, would be enough to explore the boundaries of science, I drove the shovel forcefully into the ground with my right foot, filling the head gardener's tub with soil, as he shouted, with a weary, gruff voice, "Doctor, where's your focus?"

Though I hadn't yet earned my PhD degree, they called me "Doctor" there, sometimes even asking medical questions! While I was utterly ignorant of the human body's mysteries, I fancied myself capable of answering profound cosmic questions with ease. I led several volunteer groups deployed to underprivileged areas to aid in the development of rural communities, aiming for sustainable growth through a facilitative approach. Due to a shortage of manpower, besides managerial jobs, I took on logistical, technical, and manual tasks. Our motto was "By the people, with the people, for the people." These all unfolded while my papers were under review in one of the most prestigious journals in cosmology, *JCAP* (Journal of Cosmology and Astroparticle Physics).

I could never have imagined that I would soon look back on this chapter of my life, despite its hardships, with fondness, calling it the best period of my life. As I reflect, I realize the achievements of that time have become a pillar of my awareness, forming the foundation upon which my experiences are built.

Scene Three: Returning Through a Detour

During my master's studies, I was fascinated by philosophical questions related to physics, such as:

- Is the universe inherently probabilistic at the quantum level, or is this simply a limitation of our knowledge? *(Quantum Physics)*
- If time began at the moment of the Big Bang, what existed before it? *(Cosmological Physics)*

Toward the end of my master's studies, I realized that philosophy alone wouldn't sustain my livelihood. In addition, observing my peers excel in both theoretical and experimental physics, I felt ashamed when addressing philosophical questions, and became more pessimistic about my own interests. This prompted me to choose gravitational and cosmological physics for my PhD. During this period, I shifted from the 'why' of philosophical inquiry to the 'how' of fundamental physics, dedicating myself to discovery and exploring cosmic phenomena using modern observational tools like the Planck telescope[1]. My method was structured: define the goal, persevere, and investigate thoroughly until success was achieved.[2]

My doctoral dissertation focused on cosmic microwave background radiation.[3] I studied photons[4]—quanta of light—that have traveled from the depths of space, originating from a realm that was profoundly opaque before their release.

My strategy paid off—I distanced myself from philosophical inquiries and, like my peers, achieved success. After defending my dissertation, I became a distinguished researcher, spending over five years as a postdoctoral fellow and senior postdoc at the SoA at IPM. During this time, through collaborations with

---

1. The Planck telescope was the third and last large space telescope dedicated to studying cosmic background radiation, yielding more accurate measurements of the age, geometry, and composition of the universe.
2. Rose-Agi Agas, T. (n.d.). *The Black Horse* (Bahram Pour, P., Trans.).
3. Cosmic background radiation is a radiation that uniformly fills all space. This radiation, which was accidentally discovered in 1965, is considered one of the pieces of evidence for the existence of the Big Bang.
4. In the quantum approach, light is assumed to be composed of particles called photons. Photons have no mass and always move at the speed of light.

Professor Hassan Firouzjahi, the then head of the research institute, I made good professional and occupational progress and achieved all that I had previously imagined for myself: I had an office with good access to the internet and a fairly suitable computer that I could carry out my calculations without any problem. I was satisfied with what I had and tried to do my job in the best possible way, which led to a good professional advancement.

With financial struggles easing and experiences from my research trips abroad, a new awareness unfolded within me. It was as if new knowledge was being uploaded into my mind. I could peek into my entire past and future from the branches of a plum tree, observe events in a different way, revive the questions I had covered up, and even dress my buried interests in a new attire. The philosophical questions I had abandoned—those tied to physics and cosmology—returned with renewed purpose. Their direction shifted: Why is the universe comprehensible? Why is the human mind capable of understanding it? My inquiries shifted from the cosmos to the depths of human existence. Who is man, and what latent abilities does he possess? How can he achieve maximum growth and fulfillment? Where does his actual capacity for greatness lie? I had abandoned philosophy out of shame for thinking philosophically, yet I returned to it - more philosophical than ever! Personal development and positive psychology began to captivate my interest, leading me to pursue this field.

Reflecting back, I can justify and confirm my behavior, though I know this isn't necessarily right. It reassures me that my time was not wasted. Driven by the era's demands, I redirected my life from master's studies to a doctorate, transitioning from the philosophy of the cosmos to cosmological physics. Yet, I eventually returned to philosophy, this time through the lens of humanity's deepest existential questions. This transformation allowed me to return to the right path with greater strength.

The ability to explore different paths—making seemingly contradictory choices in response to changing circumstances—is an art that fosters growth and fulfillment. I can distill this realization into a lesson: Don't stubbornly cling to a single idea or passion. If it is significant to you, let it remain in your mind, revisit it, examine it, and embrace it again when the moment feels right.

The second lesson I've learned is this: you must learn to play with the pieces before you, rather than constantly eyeing the ones others hold. Throughout my life, I gradually learned that my true strength lay in making the most of what was already in my hands. If I couldn't play my pieces well, no other pieces—no matter how tempting—would change the outcome. Over time, I saw that when new pieces are truly needed, they find their way to you at the right moment, only if you've shown your ability to play wisely with what you have.

The beautiful irony is that you can shape the game's rules while playing your pieces. You can set the terms to ensure you keep moving forward—maybe even winning on your terms. But there are no guarantees when playing someone else's game.

How a new piece is added to the game is a fundamental question. For instance, one person flourishes completely by chance, another becomes associated with a specific person, another has good genes, another has been in a good place at a specific time, and so on. However, I believe that all these opportunities can be harnessed through benevolence and helping fellow humans.

The Final Scene: A Purpose Beyond Knowledge

The profound joy I experienced in helping others during my pre-doctoral years in underprivileged areas surpasses any joy I have known. For over five years, I dedicated myself to research as a postdoctoral fellow and later as a senior postdoctoral researcher at SoA. During this time, I attended numerous international conferences and had the privilege of delivering lectures at prestigious universities worldwide. Yet, what I did for villagers, where I saw hope and joy light up their faces, brought a different delight. I have spent time with the world's greatest physicists and researchers, had teatimes[1] with them, but empathy and sharing a meal with those who were living in the worst economic conditions had a different taste.

I believe that the heartfelt prayers of those I sought to help have had a profound impact on my scientific journey. However, this does not diminish the tireless efforts of researchers worldwide.

---

1. The time between speeches at a conference when presenters and attendees engage in conversation and ask questions under the pretext of snacking and having a meal.

Their contributions to the advancement of humanity across all branches of science are undeniable. I want to say that my sense of purpose, value, impact, happiness, and the ability to bring joy to others was most profoundly realized when I was helping ordinary people, not when delivering presentations or lectures to the world's leading scientists. Although scientific fulfillment delights me, the true happiness lies elsewhere.

When I look back at the winding path of my life – from remote villages to prominent research institutions, from cosmic questions to internal inquiries – I now realize that this journey was not merely a scientific or intellectual voyage. It was a human journey, seeking flourishing in the face of uncertainty. Flourishing, I've learned, comes not from certainty, but from the courage to live fully with doubt. My experiences in various fields and the roles I have played as a father, researcher, and coach all have roots in a perspective beyond survival: a commitment to meaningful living, creating impact, and helping others find light in their lives. I have now learned that flourishing is not a final destination, but a continuous practice – a long-term commitment to growth, meaning, and courage for transformation, even when the path is unknown.

The Star I Couldn't Find in the Sky
From Cosmic Questions to Inner Light: A Journey toward Flourishing

About the Author

Dr. Alireza Talebian holds a PhD in Physics, specializing in Astronomy and Gravity, from the University of Tehran. He is a graduate of the High-Performance Master Trainer Program (for individuals and organizations), certified by the International Coaching Federation, and currently a professional coaching student at the North Star Academy. Alireza founded the Innerstellar Group, where he helps others discover their path to personal flourishing. He and his team believe that the solution to all problems lies within everyone; it is only necessary for them to better understand themselves and their inner talents (inner stars).

Alireza's life journey spans an impressive range of experiences—from studying and teaching at top Iranian universities to working in diverse fields such as baking, construction, and agriculture. He has served as a private tutor, university lecturer, and regional journalist, contributing to addiction prevention initiatives in urban areas and leading sustainable development projects in rural communities. Additionally, he has been involved in identifying and nurturing talent among elementary school children. His range of experiences is not only vast but also profound.

Alireza's initial mission was to teach physics to students and enthusiasts. Along this path, he has taught at top universities in Iran, such as the University of Tehran and Shahid Beheshti University. He has also focused on talent scouting for elementary school students by founding the Golden Magic School in Ashkezar County in Iran. He has incorporated science outreach and promotion programs into the agenda of his school activities.

With the support of his father, mother, and wife, Alireza completed his university studies in the philosophical foundations of quantum physics and cosmic radiation at reputable universities.[1] He then collaborated as a postdoctoral researcher, senior postdoctoral researcher, and full-time researcher at the School of Astronomy (SoA) at the Institute for Research in Fundamental Sciences (IPM). During these

---

1. Sharif University of Technology and the University of Tehran, Iran

collaborations, Alireza published numerous articles in top physics and cosmology journals and attracted multiple research grants.[1] He was also invited to speak and collaborate at various universities and international conferences, from Japan[2] to France[3], Spain[4], Italy[5], Switzerland[6], and Rwanda[7].

After achieving these successes, the questions Alireza had distanced himself from returned in a new shape. These questions, alongside his experience of empathy with his students, led him to take his ability to help others more seriously and contemplate launching his business; thus, Innerstellar was born.

Now that Alireza has discovered his life mission, he wants to help others achieve their dreams. He believes this lifestyle is the only path that will bring happiness and a sense of being alive to him. These days, Alireza grapples with challenges—foremost among them, transforming his professional identity from an international researcher to a successful entrepreneur.

---

1. Iran National Elite Foundation (INEF) and Iran Science Elites Federation (ISEF)
2. Yukawa Institute for Theoretical Physics (YITP)
3. Paris Institute of Astrophysics (IAP)
4. Institut de Ciències del Cosmos - Universitat de Barcelona (ICCUB)
5. The Abdus Salam International Centre for Theoretical Physics (ICTP)
6. Bernoulli Center for Fundamental Studies
7. The East African Institute for Fundamental Research (ICTP-EAIFR)

Ways to contact the author:

🌐 www.alirezatalebian.ir
in www.linkedin.com/in/innerstellar
⊙ innerstellar.me

Published by North Star Success Inc.

 www.northstarsuccess.com

 support@northstarsuccess.com

 +1 647 479 0790

Write, publish and market your book with us!

We are experts in publishing with over 20 years of experience in the industry. We will help you bring your book to life and get maximum visibility, credibility and profitability with your book.

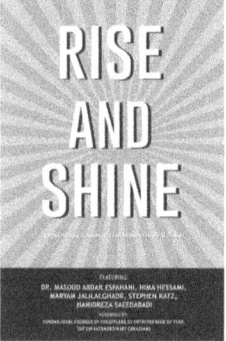

www.ingramcontent.com/pod-product-compliance
Lightning Source LLC
Chambersburg PA
CBHW061218070526
44584CB00029B/3885